Heartwarming
Soups

SEAFOOD CIOPPINO
PAGE 76

RDA ENTHUSIAST BRANDS, LLC
MILWAUKEE, WI

Heartwarming Soups

EDITORIAL
EDITOR-IN-CHIEF Catherine Cassidy
CREATIVE DIRECTOR Howard Greenberg
EDITORIAL OPERATIONS DIRECTOR Kerri Balliet

MANAGING EDITOR/PRINT & DIGITAL BOOKS Mark Hagen
ASSOCIATE CREATIVE DIRECTOR Edwin Robles Jr.

ASSOCIATE EDITOR Molly Jasinski
ART DIRECTOR Nancy Novak
EDITORIAL PRODUCTION MANAGER Dena Ahlers
COPY CHIEF Deb Warlaumont Mulvey
COPY EDITOR Mary C. Hanson
CONTRIBUTING COPY EDITOR Valerie Phillips

CHIEF FOOD EDITOR Karen Berner
FOOD EDITORS James Schend; Peggy Woodward, RD
RECIPE EDITORS Mary King; Annie Rundle; Jenni Sharp, RD; Irene Yeh
CONTENT OPERATIONS MANAGER Colleen King
CONTENT OPERATIONS ASSISTANT Shannon Stroud
EXECUTIVE ASSISTANT Marie Brannon

TEST KITCHEN & FOOD STYLING MANAGER Sarah Thompson
TEST COOKS Nicholas Iverson (lead), Matthew Hass, Lauren Knoelke
FOOD STYLISTS Kathryn Conrad (senior), Shannon Roum, Leah Rekau
PREP COOKS Megumi Garcia, Melissa Hansen, Bethany Van Jacobson, Sara Wirtz

PHOTOGRAPHY DIRECTOR Stephanie Marchese
PHOTOGRAPHERS Dan Roberts, Jim Wieland
PHOTOGRAPHER/SET STYLIST Grace Natoli Sheldon
SET STYLISTS Stacey Genaw, Melissa Haberman, Dee Dee Jacq

EDITORIAL BUSINESS MANAGER Kristy Martin

BUSINESS
VICE PRESIDENT, CHIEF SALES OFFICER Mark S. Josephson
VICE PRESIDENT, BUSINESS DEVELOPMENT & MARKETING Alain Begun
GENERAL MANAGER, TASTE OF HOME COOKING SCHOOL Erin Puariea

VICE PRESIDENT, DIGITAL EXPERIENCE & E-COMMERCE Jennifer Smith

THE READER'S DIGEST ASSOCIATION, INC.
PRESIDENT AND CHIEF EXECUTIVE OFFICER Bonnie Kintzer
VICE PRESIDENT, CHIEF OPERATING OFFICER, NORTH AMERICA Howard Halligan
VICE PRESIDENT, ENTHUSIAST BRANDS, BOOKS & RETAIL Harold Clarke
VICE PRESIDENT, NORTH AMERICAN OPERATIONS Philippe Cloutier

CHIEF MARKETING OFFICER Leslie Dukker Doty
VICE PRESIDENT, BRAND MARKETING Beth Gorry
VICE PRESIDENT, NORTH AMERICAN HUMAN RESOURCES Phyllis E. Gebhardt, SPHR
VICE PRESIDENT, CONSUMER MARKETING PLANNING Jim Woods

COVER PHOTOGRAPHY
PHOTOGRAPHER Rob Hagen
FOOD STYLIST Kaitlyn Besasie
SET STYLIST Deone Jahnke

PICTURED ON THE FRONT COVER (clockwise): Hamburger Minestrone (p. 16); Grandma's Chicken 'n' Dumpling Soup (p. 20); New Orleans Gumbo (p. 31)

PICTURED ON THE BACK COVER (from top): Loaded Baked Potato Soup (p. 7(); Bart's Black Bean Soup for Two (p. 102); Bulgur Chili (p. 60)

Soup's On!

It's time to dive into the soul-soothing goodness of homemade soup. Let *Taste of Home Heartwarming Soups* be your source for comforting classics and new favorites alike.

This brand-new collection offers sensational soups that fit any need, menu or season. Serve hearty **Cheeseburger Chowder** (p. 7) when winter winds blow, and welcome spring with a bowl of **Day After Easter Soup** (p. 80). Beating the summer sun has never been so tasty as when chilled **Watermelon Gazpacho** (p. 59) is on the menu, and **Beef & Potato Soup** (p. 9) makes a satisfying finale to any crisp autumn day.

You'll also put your slow cooker to good use since *Heartwarming Soups* includes 35 recipes for set-it and forget-it days. After all, you really can't go wrong with **Spicy Turkey Kielbasa Soup** (p. 64), **Hearty Beef & Bean Chili** (p. 63) and **Mushroom Barley Soup** (p. 72). Each comes together easily in the slow cooker, and all three are guaranteed to be hits with your family.

If you're not expecting a big crowd, turn to the chapter "Soups for Two." There you'll find delightful recipes that suit small households. Try **Creamy Butternut Squash Soup** (p. 101), **Salmon Chowder** (p. 104) or **Lentil Soup for the Soul** (p. 98) and you won't have to hassle with leftovers.

Keep an eye out for the **5-Ingredient icon** as well. It highlights recipes that use under six ingredients—talk about making dinner simple! We don't count ingredients such as salt, pepper, water and similar items you can find in the kitchen any time, so keep that in mind as you check out these appealing options.

From **Au Gratin Chicken Chowder** (p. 19) to **Zesty Steak Chili** (p. 15), these soups promise all of the taste you crave without the hassle you avoid. So call your family to the dinner table, and ladle out a little comfort tonight with *Taste of Home Heartwarming Soups*.

POTATO AND LEEK SOUP
PAGE 72

ITALIAN BEEF BARLEY STEW
PAGE 8

CURRY CHICKEN SOUP FOR TWO
PAGE 102

VEGGIE TORTELLINI SOUP
PAGE 53

PEPPERONI PIZZA CHILI
PAGE 48

Table of Contents

CREAM OF TOMATO SOUP
PAGE 89

Beef & Ground Beef

8   15   12

From ground beef and steak to meatballs and brisket, you can't deny the **hearty goodness** beef lends to soup. Whether you're craving a hamburger chowder, meaty chili, loaded-up minestrone or beef barley stew, you'll find the **perfect recipe** to satisfy and share with others here.

ZESTY HAMBURGER SOUP

Zesty Hamburger Soup

Your midday meal will keep you going right through to dinnertime when you serve my soup. Freeze leftovers in small batches so you can enjoy it anytime.

—**KELLY MILAN** LAKE JACKSON, TX

START TO FINISH: 30 MIN.
MAKES: 10 SERVINGS (3¾ QUARTS)

- 1 **pound lean ground beef (90% lean)**
- 2 **cups sliced celery**
- 1 **cup chopped onion**
- 2 **teaspoons minced garlic**
- 4 **cup water**
- 2 **medium red potatoes, peeled and cubed**
- 2 **cups frozen corn**
- 1½ **cups uncooked small shell pasta**
- 4 **pickled jalapeno slices, chopped**
- 4 **cups V8 juice**
- 2 **cans (10 ounces each) diced tomatoes with green chilies**
- 1 **to 2 tablespoons sugar**

1. In a Dutch oven, cook the beef, celery and onion over medium heat until meat is no longer pink. Add garlic; cook 1 minute longer. Drain. Stir in the water, potatoes, corn, pasta and jalapeno.

2. Bring to a boil. Reduce heat; cover and simmer for 10-15 minutes or until pasta is tender. Add the remaining ingredients; cook and stir soup until heated through.

Cheeseburger Chowder

On blustery days, my family requests this fast, meaty chowder. Serve it with oven-fresh corn bread or biscuits for a filling meal.

—**REBECCA MCCABE** EKALAKA, MT

START TO FINISH: 30 MIN.
MAKES: 7 SERVINGS

- 1 **pound ground beef**
- ¼ **cup chopped onion**
- 1½ **cups water**
- 3 **teaspoons beef bouillon granules**
- ½ **teaspoon salt**
- 2 **cups cubed red potatoes**
- 1 **celery rib, thinly sliced**
- 3 **tablespoons all-purpose flour**
- 2½ **cups milk, divided**
- 1 **cup (4 ounces) shredded cheddar cheese**

1. In a large saucepan, cook beef and onion over medium heat until meat is no longer pink; drain. Stir in the water, bouillon and salt. Add potatoes and

celery. Bring to a boil. Reduce heat; cover and simmer for 15-20 minutes or until potatoes are tender.

2. Combine flour and ½ cup milk until smooth; gradually stir into the beef mixture. Bring to a boil; cook and stir for 2 minutes or until thickened and bubbly. Stir in the remaining milk; heat through. Stir in cheese until melted.

Steak Soup

Let this thick soup simmer for awhile, and it'll be ready before you know it.

—**MARY DICE** CHEMAINUS, BC

PREP: 20 MIN. • **COOK:** 1¾ HOURS
MAKES: 6 SERVINGS

- 2 **tablespoons butter**
- 2 **tablespoons canola oil**
- 1½ **to 2 pounds beef eye round roast, cut into ½-inch cubes**
- ¼ **cup chopped onion**
- 3 **tablespoons all-purpose flour**
- 1 **tablespoon paprika**
- 1 **teaspoon salt**
- ¼ **teaspoon pepper**
- 4 **cups beef stock or broth**
- 2 **cups water**
- 1 **bay leaf**
- 4 **sprigs fresh parsley, chopped**
- 2 **sprigs celery leaves, chopped**
- ½ **teaspoon dried marjoram**
- 1½ **cups cubed peeled potatoes**
- 1½ **cups sliced carrots**
- 1½ **cups chopped celery**
- 1 **can (6 ounces) tomato paste**

1. In a Dutch oven, melt butter over medium heat; add oil. Brown beef and onion. Combine flour, paprika, salt and pepper; sprinkle over beef and mix well. Stir in stock and water. Add bay leaf, parsley, celery leaves and marjoram. Bring to a boil; reduce heat and simmer, covered, about 1 hour or until tender.

2. Add potatoes, carrots and celery. Simmer, covered, for 30-45 minutes or until vegetables are tender and soup begins to thicken. Stir in the tomato paste; simmer, uncovered, 15 minutes or until heated through. Discard bay leaf.

My son and I joined forces in creating this recipe for his work's chili cook-off. He proudly came home with a first-place ribbon!

—MARIE HATTRUP SPARKS, NV

Beef Brisket Chili

PREP: 30 MIN.
COOK: 15 MIN. + SIMMERING
MAKES: 10 SERVINGS (2½ QUARTS)

- 1 fresh beef brisket (2 pounds), cut into ½-inch pieces
- 1 large onion, finely chopped
- 2 tablespoons vegetable oil
- 2 cans (16 ounces each) kidney beans, rinsed and drained
- 1 pound smoked kielbasa or Polish sausage, coarsely chopped
- 1 jar (16 ounces) salsa
- 1 can (14½ ounces) diced tomatoes, undrained
- 1 can (8 ounces) tomato sauce
- 2 cans (4 ounces each) chopped green chilies
- 2 garlic cloves, minced
- 1 tablespoon chili powder
- 1 tablespoon ground cumin
- 1 teaspoon celery salt
- ¼ teaspoon salt
- ⅛ teaspoon pepper
- 2 to 3 tablespoons lemon juice
- 1½ teaspoons grated lemon peel

1. In a Dutch oven, brown beef and onion in oil in batches; drain. Stir in the beans, kielbasa, salsa, tomatoes, tomato sauce, chilies, garlic and seasonings.

2. Bring to a boil. Reduce heat; cover and simmer for 3 hours or until meat is tender. Just before serving, stir in lemon juice and peel.

NOTE *This is a fresh beef brisket, not corned beef.*

Italian Beef Barley Stew

I'm a fan of soups that can be made ahead and also freeze well. This satisfying soup delivers on both counts.

—JACQUELINE KLOESS IOWA CITY, IA

PREP: 30 MIN. • **COOK:** 1¼ HOURS
MAKES: 10 SERVINGS (3½ QUARTS)

- 1 boneless beef chuck roast (2 pounds), cut into ¾-inch cubes
- 3 medium onions, coarsely chopped
- 4 celery ribs, thinly sliced
- 3 medium carrots, halved lengthwise and thinly sliced
- 2 medium potatoes, peeled and cubed
- 2 garlic cloves, minced
- 1 can (46 ounces) tomato juice
- 1 can (28 ounces) diced tomatoes, undrained
- 1 bay leaf
- 1½ teaspoons dried marjoram
- 1½ teaspoons dried thyme
- ½ teaspoon salt
- ¼ teaspoon coarsely ground pepper
- ½ cup medium pearl barley

1. In a Dutch oven coated with cooking spray, cook beef and onions over medium heat until meat is no longer pink; drain. Stir in the celery, carrots and potatoes. Cook and stir 5 minutes or until crisp-tender. Add garlic; cook 1 minute longer.

2. Stir in the tomato juice, tomatoes, bay leaf and seasonings. Bring to a boil. Stir in barley. Reduce heat; cover and simmer for 1¼ to 1½ hours or until meat and barley are tender.

3. Discard bay leaf. After serving, cool any remaining soup; transfer to freezer containers. Freeze for up to 3 months.

ITALIAN BEEF BARLEY STEW

HOMINY BEEF CHILI

Beef & Potato Soup

Since I can set it and forget it while I'm out, this slow-cooker soup is a tradition at my house after church.
—**SHEILA HOLDERMAN** BERTHOLD, ND

PREP: 30 MIN. • **COOK:** 6½ HOURS
MAKES: 10 SERVINGS (3 QUARTS)

- 1½ **pounds lean ground beef (90% lean)**
- ¾ **cup chopped onion**
- ½ **cup all-purpose flour**
- 2 **cans (14½ ounces each) reduced-sodium chicken broth, divided**
- 5 **medium potatoes, peeled and cubed**
- 5 **medium carrots, chopped**
- 3 **celery ribs, chopped**
- 3 **teaspoons dried basil**
- 2 **teaspoons dried parsley flakes**
- 1 **teaspoon garlic powder**
- ½ **teaspoon pepper**
- 12 **ounces reduced-fat process cheese (Velveeta), cubed**
- 1½ **cups 2% milk**
- ½ **cup reduced-fat sour cream**

1. In a large skillet, cook beef and onion over medium heat until meat is no longer pink; drain. Combine flour and 1 can broth until smooth. Add to beef mixture. Bring to a boil; cook and stir for 2 minutes or until thickened.
2. Transfer to a 5-qt. slow cooker. Stir in potatoes, carrots, celery, seasonings and remaining broth. Cover and cook on low 6-8 hours or until vegetables are tender.
3. Stir in cheese and milk. Cover and cook 30 minutes longer or until the cheese is melted. Just before serving, stir in sour cream.

Hominy Beef Chili

Warm up during the cold of winter with my hearty chili. Loaded with beef, hominy and corn, it's supper in a bowl.
—**STEVE WESTPHAL** WIND LAKE, WI

PREP: 25 MIN. • **COOK:** 6 HOURS
MAKES: 8 SERVINGS (3 QUARTS)

- 2 **tablespoons canola oil**
- 1 **boneless beef chuck roast (3 to 4 pounds), cut into 1-inch pieces**
- 1 **can (15½ ounces) hominy, rinsed and drained**
- 1 **can (14½ ounces) reduced-sodium beef broth**
- 1 **can (14½ ounces) diced tomatoes, undrained**
- 1 **large sweet red pepper, finely chopped**
- ½ **cup chopped onion**
- 1 **can (4 ounces) chopped green chilies**
- 2 **garlic cloves, minced**
- 1 **tablespoon paprika**
- 1 **tablespoon chili powder**
- 2 **teaspoons ground cumin**
- ½ **teaspoon salt**
- ½ **teaspoon pepper**
- 1½ **cups frozen corn**
   Shredded cheddar cheese and sour cream, optional

1. In a large skillet, heat oil over medium heat. Brown beef in batches. Remove with a slotted spoon to a 5-qt. slow cooker; discard drippings.
2. Stir in hominy, broth, tomatoes, red pepper, onion, chilies, garlic and seasonings. Cook, covered, on low 6-7 hours or until meat is tender. Stir in corn; heat through. If desired, serve with cheese and sour cream.

CABBAGE AND BEEF SOUP

Hungarian Goulash Soup

This soup, which is similar to one my mom made years ago, is stuffed with vegetables. You won't be hungry after a big bowlful.

—JULIE POLAKOWSKI WEST ALLIS, WI

PREP: 40 MIN. • **COOK:** 2 HOURS
MAKES: 15 SERVINGS

- 1¼ **pounds beef stew meat, cut into 1-inch cubes**
- 2 **tablespoons olive oil, divided**
- 4 **medium onions, chopped**
- 6 **garlic cloves, minced**
- 2 **teaspoons paprika**
- ½ **teaspoon caraway seeds, crushed**
- ½ **teaspoon pepper**
- ¼ **teaspoon cayenne pepper**
- 1 **teaspoon salt-free seasoning blend**
- 2 **cans (14½ ounces each) reduced-sodium beef broth**
- 2 **cups cubed peeled potatoes**
- 2 **cups sliced carrots**
- 2 **cups cubed peeled rutabagas**
- 2 **cans (28 ounces each) diced tomatoes, undrained**
- 1 **large sweet red pepper, chopped**
- 1 **cup (8 ounces) fat-free sour cream**

1. In a Dutch oven over medium heat, brown beef in 1 tablespoon oil. Remove beef; drain drippings.
2. Heat remaining oil in the same pan; saute the onions and garlic for 8-10 minutes over medium heat or until lightly browned. Add the paprika, caraway, pepper, cayenne and seasoning blend; cook and stir 1 minute.
3. Return beef to pan. Add broth, potatoes, carrots and rutabagas; bring to a boil. Reduce heat; cover soup and simmer for 1½ hours or until vegetables are tender and meat is almost tender.
4. Add tomatoes and red pepper; return to a boil. Reduce heat; cover and simmer 30-40 minutes or until meat and vegetables are tender. Serve with sour cream.

Cabbage and Beef Soup

My mother introduced me to this soup. I helped my parents tend to our farm when I was growing up; now I grow most of the vegetables here in my very own garden.

—ETHEL LEDBETTER CANTON, NC

PREP: 10 MIN. • **COOK:** 70 MIN.
MAKES: 12 SERVINGS (3 QUARTS)

- 1 **pound lean ground beef (90% lean)**
- ½ **teaspoon garlic salt**
- ¼ **teaspoon garlic powder**
- ¼ **teaspoon pepper**
- 2 **celery ribs, chopped**
- 1 **can (16 ounces) kidney beans, rinsed and drained**
- ½ **medium head cabbage, chopped**
- 1 **can (28 ounces) diced tomatoes, undrained**
- 1 **tomato can water**
- 4 **teaspoons beef bouillon granules**
  Minced fresh parsley

1. In a Dutch oven, cook beef over medium heat until no longer pink; drain. Stir in the remaining ingredients except parsley.
2. Bring to a boil. Reduce heat; cover and simmer for 1 hour. Garnish with the parsley.

Cheeseburger Soup with Rice

I don't have a lot of extra time to spend in the kitchen, so I appreciate that I can cook the ground beef and rice in advance to speed up the prep work on busy days.

—**JANNE ROWE** WICHITA, KS

START TO FINISH: 30 MIN.
MAKES: 10 SERVINGS (ABOUT 2½ QUARTS)

- 1 **cup shredded carrot**
- 1 **cup chopped onion**
- ½ **cup chopped celery**
- 2 **cans (14½ ounces each) chicken broth**
- 1 **pound ground beef, cooked, crumbled and drained**
- 2 **cups cooked long grain rice**
- 3 **cups milk**
- 1 **pound process cheese (Velveeta), cubed**
- 1 **cup (8 ounces) sour cream**

1. In a large saucepan, combine the carrot, onion, celery and broth. Bring to a boil. Reduce heat; simmer, uncovered, for 15 minutes or until vegetables are tender.
2. Stir in the beef, rice, milk and cheese; simmer, uncovered, until cheese is melted, stirring occasionally (do not boil). Just before serving, whisk in the sour cream; heat through.

Tortilla Soup

Because my whole family likes Mexican food, we find this soup especially appealing. It has just the right amount of zip without being overwhelming.

—**TAMMY LEIBER** NAVASOTA, TX

PREP: 20 MIN. • **COOK:** 1¾ HOURS
MAKES: 10 SERVINGS (2½ QUARTS)

- 1 **medium onion, chopped**
- 2 **tablespoons canola oil**
- 2 **garlic cloves, minced**
- 2 **pounds beef stew meat, cut into 1-inch cubes**
- 2 **cups water**
- 1 **can (14½ ounces) stewed tomatoes**
- 1 **can (10 ounces) diced tomatoes with green chilies, undrained**
- 1 **can (10¾ ounces) condensed tomato soup, undiluted**
- 1 **can (10½ ounces) beef broth**
- 1 **can (10½ ounces) chicken broth**
- 1 **tablespoon Worcestershire sauce**
- 1 **teaspoon ground cumin**
- 1 **teaspoon chili powder**
- 1 **teaspoon salt**
- 1 **teaspoon lemon-pepper seasoning**
- ½ **teaspoon hot pepper sauce**
- 10 **corn tortillas (6 inches)**
  Shredded cheddar cheese, sour cream and sliced green onions, optional

1. In a Dutch oven, saute onion in oil until tender. Add garlic; cook 1 minute longer. Stir in the next 13 ingredients; bring to a boil. Reduce heat; cover and simmer for 1½ hours or until beef is tender.
2. Tear tortillas into bite-size pieces; add to soup. Simmer, uncovered, for 10 minutes; let stand for 5 minutes. Garnish individual servings with cheese, sour cream and onions if desired.

TORTILLA SOUP

ROASTED POBLANO BEEF STEW

Roasted Poblano Beef Stew

I like to keep my son's heritage alive through cooking, and this recipe reflects my wife's Hispanic background. She gave it high praise when I presented it!

—GREG FONTENOT THE WOODLANDS, TX

PREP: 40 MIN. + STANDING
COOK: 2 HOURS
MAKES: 8 SERVINGS (3 QUARTS)

- 5 **poblano peppers**
- 1 **boneless beef chuck roast (2 to 3 pounds), cut into 1-inch cubes**
- 2 **tablespoons olive oil**
- 1 **medium onion, chopped**
- 3 **garlic cloves, minced**
- 1 **carton (32 ounces) beef broth**
- 2 **medium tomatoes, chopped**
- ⅓ **cup minced fresh cilantro**
- 1 **tablespoon chili powder**
- 1 **teaspoon salt**
- 1 **teaspoon ground cumin**
- ½ **teaspoon pepper**
- 2 **large potatoes, peeled and cut into 1-inch cubes**

1. Broil poblano peppers 4 in. from the heat until skins blister, about 5 minutes. With tongs, rotate peppers a quarter turn. Broil and rotate until all sides are blistered and blackened. Immediately place poblanos in a small bowl; cover and let stand for 20 minutes.
2. Peel off and discard charred skins. Remove stems and seeds. Coarsely chop poblanos.

3. In a Dutch oven, brown beef in oil in batches. Remove and keep warm. In the same pan, saute onion until tender. Add garlic; cook 1 minute longer.
4. Gradually add broth; stir in the tomatoes, cilantro, chili powder, salt, cumin, pepper, poblanos and beef. Bring to a boil. Reduce heat; cover and simmer 1½ hours or until beef is tender. Add the potatoes; cook 10-15 minutes longer or until the potatoes are tender. Skim fat.

Hearty Hamburger Soup

This thick soup, full of beef, veggies and noodles, satisfies my husband's appetite after a busy day on the farm.

—JULIE GREEN HULL, IA

PREP: 10 MIN. • **COOK:** 30 MIN.
MAKES: 12 SERVINGS (3 QUARTS)

- 2 **pounds ground beef**
- ½ **cup chopped onion**
- 6 **cups water**
- 1 **package (10 ounces) frozen mixed vegetables**
- 1 **can (14½ ounces) diced tomatoes, undrained**
- 1 **package (6¾ ounces) beef pasta dinner mix**
- 1 **bay leaf**
- ¼ **to ½ teaspoon salt**
- ¼ **teaspoon pepper**

In a Dutch oven, cook beef and onion over medium heat until meat is no longer pink; drain. Stir in remaining ingredients; bring to a boil. Reduce heat; cover and simmer until pasta is tender. Discard bay leaf.

Meatball Minestrone

Just thinking about this soup simmering on the stove gets me hungry! The homemade meatballs are so tasty.

—ESTHER PEREA VAN NUYS, CA

PREP: 30 MIN. • **COOK:** 45 MIN.
MAKES: 8 SERVINGS (2 QUARTS)

- 1 **pound ground beef**
- 1 **egg, lightly beaten**
- ½ **cup chopped onion**
- ¼ **cup dry bread crumbs**
- 1 **teaspoon salt**
- ¼ **teaspoon pepper**
- 1 **can (15 ounces) tomato sauce**
- 2½ **cups water**
- 1 **can (15½ ounces) kidney beans with liquid**
- ½ **teaspoon dried oregano**
- ¼ **teaspoon dried thyme**
- 1 **cup sliced celery**
- ¼ **cup uncooked elbow macaroni**
- ¼ **cup chopped fresh parsley**

1. In a large bowl, combine the beef, egg, onion, crumbs, salt and pepper. Shape into 1-in. balls.
2. In a large saucepan, brown the meatballs on all sides until no longer pink. Drain. Add the remaining ingredients except macaroni and parsley; cover and simmer 20 minutes. Add macaroni; simmer 10 minutes or until tender. Stir in parsley.

For meatballs to **cook evenly,** it's important they be the same size. The easiest way to ensure uniformity? Use a 1- or 1½-inch **cookie scoop.**

MEATBALL MINESTRONE

Potluck Pasta Soup

Expect friends and family to show up early when you announce this Italian restaurant-inspired soup is on the menu.
—**MARILYN FOSS** BEAVERTOWN, OH

PREP: 15 MIN. • **COOK:** 1 HOUR 25 MIN.
MAKES: 20 SERVINGS (5 QUARTS)

- 1½ **pounds ground beef**
- 8 **cups water**
- 2 **cans (14½ ounces each) Italian stewed tomatoes**
- 2 **cups diced carrots**
- 1½ **cups diced celery**
- 1 **cup chopped onion**
- ½ **cup chopped green pepper**
- 1 **can (8 ounces) tomato sauce**
- 1 **envelope onion soup mix**
- 1 **tablespoon sugar**
- 1 **teaspoon Italian seasoning**
- 2 **garlic cloves, minced**
- 2 **bay leaves**
- ½ **teaspoon pepper**
- 3 **cups cooked elbow macaroni**
- 1 **can (15 ounces) garbanzo beans or chickpeas, rinsed and drained**

1. In a stockpot, cook beef over medium heat until no longer pink; drain. Add the water, tomatoes, carrots, celery, onion, green pepper, tomato sauce, soup mix, sugar and seasonings; bring to a boil. Reduce heat; simmer, uncovered, for 1 hour.

2. Stir in macaroni and beans; heat through. Discard bay leaves.

NOTE *To reduce preparation time when making Potluck Pasta Soup, chop the carrots, celery and onion early in the day or the night before. Store vegetables in separate plastic bags in the refrigerator.*

Lasagna Soup

Lasagna in a bowl? Believe it! All the flavors of lasagna come together in this heartwarming one-dish meal.
—**SHERYL OLENICK** DEMAREST, NJ

START TO FINISH: 30 MIN.
MAKES: 8 SERVINGS (2¾ QUARTS)

- 1 **pound lean ground beef (90% lean)**
- 1 **large green pepper, chopped**
- 1 **medium onion, chopped**
- 2 **garlic cloves, minced**
- 2 **cans (14½ ounces each) diced tomatoes, undrained**
- 2 **cans (14½ ounces each) reduced-sodium beef broth**
- 1 **can (8 ounces) tomato sauce**
- 1 **cup frozen corn**
- ¼ **cup tomato paste**
- 2 **teaspoons Italian seasoning**
- ¼ **teaspoon pepper**
- 2½ **cups uncooked spiral pasta**
- ½ **cup shredded Parmesan cheese**

1. In a large saucepan, cook beef, green pepper and onion over medium heat 6-8 minutes or until meat is no longer pink, breaking up beef into crumbles. Add garlic; cook 1 minute longer. Drain.

2. Stir in tomatoes, broth, tomato sauce, corn, tomato paste, Italian seasoning and pepper. Bring to a boil. Stir in pasta. Return to a boil. Reduce heat; simmer, covered, 10-12 minutes or until pasta is tender. Sprinkle soup with cheese.

German Vegetable Soup

My sister-in-law gave me the recipe for this thick soup. Don't let the long list of ingredients scare you off—the flavor is worth the extra effort.

—**GUDRUN BRAKER** BURNETT, WI

PREP: 15 MIN. • **COOK:** 35 MIN.
MAKES: 16 SERVINGS (4 QUARTS)

- 1½ pounds ground beef
- 2 medium onions, diced
- 2 tablespoons beef bouillon granules
- 1 cup water
  Salt and pepper to taste
- ½ to 1 teaspoon garlic powder
- 1 bay leaf
- 1 can (46 ounces) tomato or vegetable juice
- 3 celery ribs, diced
- 6 medium carrots, sliced
- 3 medium potatoes, peeled and diced
- 3 cups shredded cabbage
- 1 small green pepper, chopped
- 1 can (15¼ ounces) whole kernel corn, drained
- 1 can (8½ ounces) peas, drained
- 1 can (8 ounces) cut green beans, drained

1. In a Dutch oven, cook beef and onions over medium heat until meat is no longer pink; drain.
2. Dissolve the bouillon in water; add to the beef mixture. Add salt, pepper, garlic, bay leaf, tomato juice, celery, carrots, potatoes, cabbage and green pepper.
3. Simmer, uncovered, for 25 minutes or until vegetables are tender. Stir in the corn, peas and beans; heat through. Discard bay leaf before serving.

Zesty Steak Chili

This Texas-style chili tastes even better the second day. If you're lucky enough to make it last that long.

—**MICHELLE SMITH** RUNNING SPRINGS, CA

PREP: 40 MIN. • **COOK:** 2 HOURS
MAKES: 20 SERVINGS

- 4 pounds beef top round steak, cut into 1-inch cubes
- 4 garlic cloves, minced
- ¼ cup canola oil
- 3 cups chopped onion
- 2¾ cups water, divided
- 2 cups sliced celery
- 3 cans (14½ ounces each) diced tomatoes, undrained
- 2 cans (15 ounces each) no-salt-added tomato sauce
- 1 jar (16 ounces) salsa
- 3 tablespoons chili powder
- 2 teaspoons ground cumin
- 2 teaspoons dried oregano
- 1 teaspoon salt, optional
- 1 teaspoon pepper
- ¼ cup all-purpose flour
- ¼ cup yellow cornmeal
  Shredded reduced-fat cheddar cheese, reduced-fat sour cream, sliced green onions and sliced ripe olives, optional

1. In a Dutch oven over medium-high heat, saute steak and garlic in oil until browned. Add onion; cook and stir for 5 minutes. Stir in 2 cups water and next nine ingredients; bring to a boil.
2. Reduce heat; cover and simmer 2 hours or until tender. Combine flour, cornmeal and remaining water; stir until smooth. Bring chili to a boil. Add flour mixture; cook and stir 2 minutes or until thickened. If desired, garnish with reduced-fat cheese, reduced-fat sour cream, onions and olives.

ZESTY STEAK CHILI

Hamburger Minestrone

Any frozen mixed vegetables, in addition to whatever small pasta you have on hand, will work well in this dish.
—TASTE OF HOME TEST KITCHEN

START TO FINISH: 30 MIN.
MAKES: 6 SERVINGS

- ½ cup uncooked small pasta shells
- 1 pound ground beef
- ½ cup chopped onion
- 3 cans (14½ ounces each) beef broth
- 1 package (16 ounces) frozen mixed vegetables
- 1 can (16 ounces) kidney beans, rinsed and drained
- 1 can (14½ ounces) diced tomatoes, undrained
- 1 can (6 ounces) tomato paste
- 3 teaspoons Italian seasoning
- 1 teaspoon salt
- ¼ teaspoon dried thyme
- ¼ teaspoon dried basil
- ¼ teaspoon pepper

1. Cook pasta according to package directions. Meanwhile, in a large saucepan, cook beef and onion over medium heat until meat is no longer pink; drain.

2. Stir in the remaining ingredients. Bring to a boil. Reduce heat; simmer, uncovered, for 15 minutes. Drain pasta and add to pan; heat through.

HEARTY PUMPKIN CHILI WITH POLENTA

Hearty Pumpkin Chili with Polenta

If you want, make this healthy chili a day ahead. It reheats very nicely, and the polenta keeps in the fridge for a few days—just make sure you store it in an airtight container.
—WENDY RUSCH TREGO, WI

PREP: 30 MIN. • **COOK:** 45 MIN.
MAKES: 6 SERVINGS

- 1 pound ground beef
- 2 celery ribs, finely chopped
- 1 medium onion, finely chopped
- 1 small sweet red pepper, finely chopped
- 2 garlic cloves, minced
- 1 can (29 ounces) tomato sauce
- 1 can (15 ounces) crushed tomatoes
- 1 can (15 ounces) solid-pack pumpkin
- 1 tablespoon plus 2 teaspoons sugar, divided
- 1 tablespoon chili powder
- 1½ teaspoons pumpkin pie spice
- ½ teaspoon plus ¾ teaspoon salt, divided
- ½ teaspoon pepper
- 1½ cups 2% milk
- ½ cup heavy whipping cream
- ¼ cup butter, cubed
- ¾ cup yellow cornmeal
- 1 can (15 ounces) black beans, rinsed and drained

1. In a Dutch oven, cook the first five ingredients over medium heat for 8-10 minutes or until beef is no longer pink and vegetables are tender, breaking up beef into crumbles; drain.

2. Stir in tomato sauce, tomatoes, pumpkin, 1 tablespoon sugar, chili powder, pie spice, ½ teaspoon salt and pepper; bring to a boil. Reduce heat; simmer, uncovered, 45 minutes, stirring occasionally.

3. Meanwhile, in a large heavy saucepan, bring milk, cream, butter, and remaining sugar and salt to a boil. Reduce heat to a gentle boil; slowly whisk in cornmeal. Cook and stir with a wooden spoon 2-3 minutes or until polenta is thickened and pulls away cleanly from sides of pan (mixture will be very thick).

4. Pour into a greased 9-in.-square baking pan. Let stand until firm, about 30 minutes.

5. Stir the beans into chili; heat through. Cut polenta into six pieces. Serve with chili.

⑤INGREDIENTS
Vegetable Meatball Soup

You can have this delicious soup on the table in under 30 minutes. If you have leftover meatballs from a previous meal, it's a great way to use them up.

—**SUSAN WESTERFIELD** ALBUQUERQUE, NM

START TO FINISH: 25 MIN.
MAKES: 6 SERVINGS (2 QUARTS)

- 1 package (12 ounces) frozen fully cooked Italian meatballs
- 2 cans (14½ ounces each) beef broth
- 2 cups frozen Italian vegetable blend
- 1 can (14½ ounces) Italian diced tomatoes, undrained
- 1½ cups water
- ⅓ cup small pasta shells
  Shredded Parmesan cheese, optional

In a Dutch oven, combine meatballs, broth, vegetable blend, tomatoes, water and pasta. Bring to a boil. Reduce heat; simmer, uncovered, for 10-12 minutes or until pasta is tender. Garnish servings with cheese if desired.

Pizza Soup

This family favorite is unlike any soup you've tried before. Sometimes I use bacon or salami in it instead of pepperoni.

—**JANET BELDMAN** LONDON, ON

PREP: 15 MIN. • **COOK:** 20 MIN.
MAKES: 6 SERVINGS

- 1 pound ground beef
- 1 small onion, chopped
- 1 cup sliced fresh mushrooms
- 1 medium green pepper, cut into strips
- 1 can (28 ounces) diced tomatoes, undrained
- 1 cup beef broth
- 1 cup sliced pepperoni
- 1 teaspoon dried basil
  Shredded mozzarella cheese

1. In a large saucepan, cook the beef, onion, mushrooms and green pepper over medium heat until meat is no longer pink and vegetables are almost tender; drain. Stir in the tomatoes, broth, pepperoni and basil. Cook until heated through.
2. Ladle into ovenproof bowls; top with cheese. Broil or microwave until cheese melts and is bubbly.

⑤INGREDIENTS
Spicy Potato Soup

My sister-in-law, who is from Mexico, passed along this wonderful recipe. Since she prefers her foods much spicier than we do, I've cut back on the heat by reducing the amount of pepper sauce, but you can add more if you prefer a bigger kick.

—**AUDREY WALL** INDUSTRY, PA

PREP: 5 MIN. • **COOK:** 1 HOUR 5 MIN.
MAKES: 6-8 SERVINGS (2 QUARTS)

- 1 pound ground beef
- 4 cups cubed peeled potatoes (½-inch cubes)
- 1 small onion, chopped
- 3 cans (8 ounces each) tomato sauce
- 4 cups water
- 2 teaspoons salt
- 1½ teaspoons pepper
- ½ to 1 teaspoon hot pepper sauce

In a Dutch oven, brown ground beef over medium heat until no longer pink; drain. Add the potatoes, onion and tomato sauce. Stir in the water, salt, pepper and hot pepper sauce; bring to a boil. Reduce heat and simmer for 1 hour or until the potatoes are tender and the soup has thickened.

VEGETABLE MEATBALL SOUP

Chicken & Turkey

When you think of soup, **the wonderful aroma** and flavor of chicken noodle soup probably come to mind. And with good reason! Turn to this chapter any time you need to **soothe the soul** as well as appetites. You can't go wrong with these classics, but you'll also find plenty of new **family favorites** as well.

Au Gratin Chicken Chowder

Everyone will want seconds of this quick and filling chowder. Canned corn and packaged potatoes make it a snap to prepare anytime.

—**ELLA EBERLY** ENGLEWOOD, OH

START TO FINISH: 30 MIN.
MAKES: 6 SERVINGS (ABOUT 2 QUARTS)

- 6 **bacon strips, diced**
- 1 **small onion, chopped**
- 1 **package (4.9 ounces) au gratin potatoes**
- 2 **cups water**
- 1½ **cups 2% milk**
- 1¼ **cups chicken broth**
- 1 **can (15¼ ounces) whole kernel corn, drained**
- 1 **bay leaf**
- 3 **cups cubed cooked chicken**
- ⅔ **cup evaporated milk**

1. In a large saucepan, cook bacon over medium heat until crisp. Remove to paper towels with a slotted spoon; drain, reserving 2 tablespoons drippings.
2. Saute onion in drippings until tender. Add the potatoes with contents of sauce mix, water, milk, broth, corn and bay leaf. Cook, uncovered, over medium heat for 15-20 minutes or until potatoes are tender, stirring occasionally.
3. Reduce heat. Stir in the chicken, evaporated milk and bacon; heat through. Discard bay leaf.

Fiesta Chorizo-Chicken Soup

Set some rolls on the table when you serve this soup and you'll have a comforting meal that'll perk you up.

—**KATHY RODENBECK** FORT WAYNE, IN

PREP: 30 MIN. • **COOK:** 35 MIN.
MAKES: 12 SERVINGS (4½ QUARTS)

- 1 **pound uncooked chorizo, casings removed, or bulk spicy pork sausage**
- 2 **cups sliced fresh carrots**
- 1 **medium onion, chopped**
- 4 **garlic cloves, minced**
- 1 **pound boneless skinless chicken breasts, cubed**
- 1 **teaspoon salt**
- ¼ **teaspoon pepper**
- 2 **tablespoons olive oil**
- 3 **medium sweet potatoes, peeled and cubed**
- 1 **package (10 ounces) frozen corn**
- 1 **medium sweet red pepper, chopped**
- 1 **carton (32 ounces) reduced-sodium chicken broth**
- 1 **can (16 ounces) butter beans, rinsed and drained**
- 1 **can (15 ounces) black beans, rinsed and drained**
- 1 **can (14½ ounces) fire-roasted diced tomatoes, undrained**
- 1 **can (5½ ounces) reduced-sodium V8 juice**
- 1 **teaspoon hot pepper sauce**
- 2 **cups fresh spinach, chopped**

1. Crumble chorizo into a Dutch oven. Add the carrots, onion and garlic. Cook over medium heat until chorizo is fully cooked. Drain; remove from pan and set aside.
2. In the same pan, saute the chicken, salt and pepper in oil until no longer pink. Add sweet potatoes, corn and red pepper; cook 5 minutes longer.
3. Stir in the chorizo mixture, broth, beans, tomatoes, V8 juice and pepper sauce. Bring to a boil. Reduce heat; simmer, uncovered, for 15 minutes or until vegetables are tender. Stir in spinach; cook until wilted.

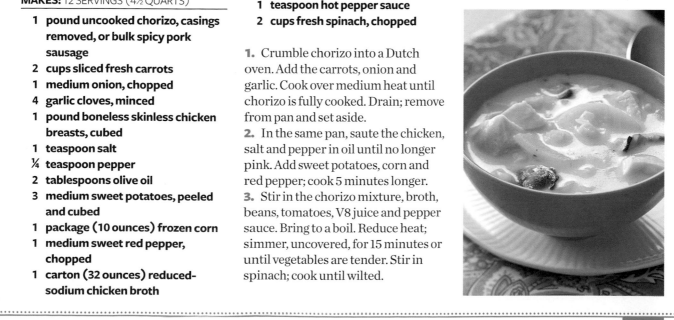

SOUTHWEST TURKEY SOUP

1½ cups chopped carrots
1 cup fresh or frozen peas
1 cup chopped celery
1 cup chopped peeled potatoes
¼ cup chopped onion
1½ teaspoons seasoned salt
¼ teaspoon pepper
1 bay leaf

DUMPLINGS

2 cups all-purpose flour
4 teaspoons baking powder
1 teaspoon salt
¼ teaspoon pepper
1 egg, beaten
2 tablespoons butter, melted
¾ to 1 cup milk
Snipped fresh parsley, optional

1. Place the chicken, water, bouillon, peppercorns and cloves in a stockpot. Cover and bring to a boil; skim foam. Reduce heat; cover and simmer 45-60 minutes or until chicken is tender. Strain broth; return to stockpot.

2. Remove chicken and set aside until cool enough to handle. Remove meat from bones; discard bones and skin and cut chicken into chunks. Cool broth and skim off fat.

3. Return chicken to stockpot with soups, vegetables and seasonings; bring to a boil. Reduce heat; cover and simmer for 1 hour. Uncover; increase heat to a gentle boil. Discard bay leaf.

4. For dumplings, combine dry ingredients in a medium bowl. Stir in egg, butter and enough milk to make a moist, stiff batter. Drop by teaspoonfuls into soup. Cover and cook without lifting the lid for 18-20 minutes. Sprinkle with parsley if desired.

Southwest Turkey Soup

Ground turkey and a few other ingredients arc all you'll need for this satisfying soup that's spiced with salsa, green chilies and chili powder. It's the perfect way to fill up when you are crunched for time.

—GENISE KRAUSE STURGEON BAY, WI

START TO FINISH: 30 MIN.
MAKES: 6 SERVINGS (2½ QUARTS)

1 pound ground turkey
1 tablespoon olive oil
2 cans (16 ounces each) kidney beans, rinsed and drained
2 cans (14½ ounces each) chicken broth
2 cups frozen corn
1 cup salsa
1 can (4 ounces) chopped green chilies
1 to 2 tablespoons chili powder
Sour cream and minced fresh cilantro

1. In a Dutch oven, cook turkey in oil over medium heat until meat is no longer pink; drain.

2. Add beans, broth, corn, salsa, chilies and chili powder. Bring to a boil. Reduce heat; cover and simmer for 10-15 minutes to allow flavors to blend. Serve with sour cream and cilantro.

Grandma's Chicken 'n' Dumpling Soup

I've enjoyed making this rich soup for 30 years. Every time I serve it, I remember my grandma, who was very special to me and was known as a great cook.

—PAULETTE BALDA PROPHETSTOWN, IL

PREP: 20 MIN. + COOLING
COOK: 2¾ HOURS
MAKES: 12 SERVINGS (3 QUARTS)

1 broiler/fryer chicken (3½ to 4 pounds), cut up
2¼ quarts cold water
5 chicken bouillon cubes
6 whole peppercorns
3 whole cloves
1 can (10¾ ounces) condensed cream of chicken soup, undiluted
1 can (10¾ ounces) condensed cream of mushroom soup, undiluted

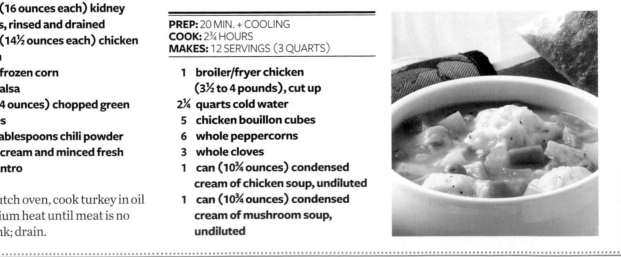

One night I didn't have any noodles for my chicken soup, so I gave it an Asian twist with wonton wrappers. It was a success! Don't skip the celery leaves; they bring great flavor to this soup.

—**NOELLE MYERS** GRAND FORKS, ND

ASIAN CHICKEN NOODLE SOUP

Asian Chicken Noodle Soup

PREP: 15 MIN. • **COOK:** 40 MIN.
MAKES: 10 SERVINGS (2½ QUARTS)

- 1½ **pounds boneless skinless chicken breasts, cut into 1-inch cubes**
- 1 **tablespoon sesame oil**
- 3 **medium carrots, sliced**
- 2 **celery ribs, chopped**
- 1 **medium onion, chopped**
- 6 **cups chicken broth**
- ⅓ **cup teriyaki sauce**
- ¼ **cup chili garlic sauce**
- 1 **package (12 ounces) wonton wrappers, cut into ¼-inch strips**
- 2 **cups sliced fresh shiitake mushrooms**
- ⅓ **cup chopped celery leaves**
- ¼ **cup minced fresh basil**
- 2 **tablespoons minced fresh cilantro**
- 2 **green onions, sliced**

1. In a Dutch oven, cook chicken in oil over medium heat until no longer pink. Remove and keep warm. In the same pan, saute the carrots, celery and onion until tender. Stir in the broth, teriyaki sauce, garlic sauce and chicken. Bring to a boil. Reduce heat; simmer, uncovered, for 20 minutes.
2. Add wonton strips, mushrooms, celery leaves, basil and cilantro. Cook and stir for 4-5 minutes or until wonton strips and mushrooms are tender. Sprinkle with green onions.

Zesty Chicken Tortellini Soup

I love it when this soup is on the menu. Don't hesitate to toss in any veggies you happen to have on hand.

—**NANCY LATULIPPE** SIMCOE, ON

PREP: 10 MIN. • **COOK:** 40 MIN.
MAKES: 6 SERVINGS (2½ QUARTS)

- 4 **cups reduced-sodium chicken broth**
- 4 **cups reduced-sodium beef broth**
- 6 **boneless skinless chicken thighs (about 1½ pounds)**
- 4 **medium carrots, sliced**
- 2 **celery ribs, sliced**
- 1 **small onion, chopped**
- 1 **envelope reduced-sodium onion soup mix**
- 1½ **teaspoons dried parsley flakes**
- ½ **teaspoon garlic powder**
- ½ **teaspoon crushed red pepper flakes**
- ½ **teaspoon poultry seasoning**
- ½ **teaspoon pepper**
- 2½ **cups frozen cheese tortellini**

1. In a Dutch oven, bring chicken broth and beef broth to a boil; reduce heat. Add chicken and poach, uncovered, for 25-30 minutes or until a thermometer reads 170°. Remove chicken; cool slightly.

2. Add the carrots, celery, onion, soup mix, parsley and seasonings to broth. Bring to a boil. Reduce heat; cover and simmer for 10-15 minutes or until vegetables are tender.

3. Meanwhile, chop chicken. Add tortellini and chicken to soup. Simmer for 5-10 minutes or until tortellini is tender.

Butternut Turkey Soup

Although it's hearty with lots of nutritious vegetables and turkey, this soup won't weigh you down.

—**DENISE LAROCHE** HUDSON, NH

PREP: 30 MIN. • **COOK:** 35 MIN.
MAKES: 6 SERVINGS (2 QUARTS)

- 3 **shallots, thinly sliced**
- 1 **teaspoon olive oil**
- 3 **cups reduced-sodium chicken broth**
- 3 **cups cubed peeled butternut squash (¾-inch cubes)**
- 2 **medium red potatoes, cut into ½-inch cubes**
- 1½ **cups water**
- 2 **teaspoons minced fresh thyme**
- ½ **teaspoon pepper**
- 2 **whole cloves**
- 3 **cups cubed cooked turkey breast**

1. In a large saucepan coated with cooking spray, cook shallots in oil over medium heat until tender. Stir in the broth, squash, potatoes, water, thyme and pepper.

2. Place cloves on a double thickness of cheesecloth; bring up corners of cloth and tie with string to form a bag. Stir into soup. Bring to a boil. Reduce heat; cover and simmer for 10-15 minutes or until vegetables are tender. Stir in turkey; heat through. Discard spice bag.

BUTTERNUT TURKEY SOUP

Turkey & Dumpling Soup

When it gets colder outside, my husband knows this soup is going to make an appearance. The recipe was handed down by my grandmother, who just happened to be a caterer.

—KAREN SUE GARBACK-PRISTERA
ALBANY, NY

PREP: 35 MIN. • **COOK:** 3 HOURS
MAKES: 6 SERVINGS (ABOUT 2 QUARTS)

- 1 leftover turkey carcass (from a 12- to 14-pound turkey)
- 9 cups water
- 3 teaspoons chicken bouillon granules
- 1 bay leaf
- 1 can (14½ ounces) stewed tomatoes, cut up
- 1 medium turnip, peeled and diced
- 2 celery ribs, chopped
- 1 medium onion, chopped
- 1 medium carrot, chopped
- ¼ cup minced fresh parsley
- 1 teaspoon salt

DUMPLINGS
- ½ cup water
- ¼ cup butter, cubed
- ½ cup all-purpose flour
- 1 teaspoon baking powder
- ⅛ teaspoon salt
- 2 eggs
- 1 tablespoon minced fresh parsley

1. Place carcass, water, bouillon and bay leaf in a stockpot. Bring to a boil. Reduce heat; cover and simmer for 1½ hours.

2. Remove carcass. Strain broth and skim fat; discard bay leaf. Return broth to pan. Add the tomatoes, vegetables, parsley and salt. Remove turkey from bones and cut into bite-size pieces; add to soup. Discard bones. Bring soup to a boil. Reduce heat; cover and simmer for 25-30 minutes or until vegetables are crisp-tender.

3. For dumplings, in a large saucepan, bring water and butter to a boil. Combine the flour, baking powder and salt; add all at once to pan and stir until a smooth ball forms. Remove from heat; let stand for 5 minutes. Add eggs, one at a time, beating well after each addition. Continue beating until mixture is smooth and shiny. Stir in parsley.

4. Drop batter in 12 mounds into simmering soup. Cover and simmer for 20 minutes or until a toothpick inserted into a dumpling comes out clean (do not lift cover while simmering).

Shrimp 'n' Chicken Noodle Soup

Give your dinner a Thai twist! You'll be amazed that something as simple as ramen noodles can create such an intriguing soup.

—TODD SCHAAL LAKE CITY, MN

START TO FINISH: 25 MIN.
MAKES: 4 SERVINGS

- ¼ cup chopped sweet onion
- 3 green onions, sliced
- 1 can (4 ounces) mushroom stems and pieces, drained
- 2 teaspoons olive oil
- 2 teaspoons minced garlic
- ¾ cup frozen cooked salad shrimp, thawed
- 1 teaspoon dried rosemary, crushed
- ¼ teaspoon lemon-pepper seasoning
- 2 cans (14½ ounces each) chicken broth
- 1 cup cubed cooked chicken
- 1 package (3 ounces) chicken ramen noodles
- 2 tablespoons crumbled cooked bacon, optional

1. In a large saucepan, saute onions and mushrooms in oil. Add the garlic; cook 1 minute longer. Stir in the shrimp, rosemary and lemon-pepper. Cook for 3-4 minutes or until vegetables are tender.

2. Stir in the broth, chicken, ramen noodles and contents of seasoning packet if desired. Bring to a boil. Reduce heat; cover and simmer for 6-8 minutes or until noodles are tender. Garnish with bacon if desired.

WHITE CHICKEN CHILI

Lime, cumin and cilantro add a nice punch to this chicken chili. It's a clever twist on the classic that you're sure to love.

—DONNA LINDECAMP MORGANTON, NC

White Chicken Chili

PREP: 25 MIN. • **COOK:** 1 HOUR
MAKES: 7 SERVINGS

- 2 **cans (14½ ounces each) chicken broth**
- 3 **bone-in chicken breast halves (8 ounces each), skin removed**
- 1 **large onion, chopped**
- 2 **garlic cloves, minced**
- 1 **teaspoon ground cumin**
- 1 **teaspoon dried oregano**
- ½ **teaspoon salt**
- ¼ **teaspoon cayenne pepper**
- 2 **cans (15½ ounces each) great northern beans, rinsed and drained**
- 1½ **cups frozen white corn**
- ⅓ **cup lime juice**
    Sour cream, shredded white cheddar cheese and/or minced fresh cilantro, optional

1. In a large saucepan, combine the first eight ingredients. Bring to a boil. Reduce heat; cover and simmer for 35-40 minutes or until a thermometer inserted into chicken reads 170°. Remove chicken from broth; allow to cool.

2. Remove meat from bones; discard bones. Cube chicken and return to pan. Mash half of the beans. Add all of the beans, corn and lime juice to chicken mixture. Return to a boil. Reduce heat; cover and simmer for 15-20 minutes or until flavors are blended.

3. Serve with sour cream, cheese and cilantro if desired.

Italian Chicken Sausage Soup

This dish bursts with fabulous Italian flavors. Your family might think you got the recipe from an upscale restaurant!

—CHERYL RAVESI MILFORD, MA

PREP: 15 MIN. • **COOK:** 40 MIN.
MAKES: 6 SERVINGS (2½ QUARTS)

- 1 **package (12 ounces) fully cooked Italian chicken sausage links, halved lengthwise and sliced**
- 1 **medium onion, chopped**
- 1 **tablespoon olive oil**
- 3 **garlic cloves, minced**
- 2 **cans (15 ounces each) white kidney or cannellini beans, rinsed and drained**
- 2 **cans (14½ ounces each) no-salt-added diced tomatoes**
- 2 **medium zucchini, quartered and sliced**
- 1 **can (14½ ounces) reduced-sodium chicken broth**
- 8 **ounces whole fresh mushrooms, quartered**
- 1 **cup water**
- ¼ **cup prepared pesto**
- ¼ **cup dry red wine or additional reduced-sodium chicken broth**
- 1 **tablespoon balsamic vinegar**
- 1 **teaspoon minced fresh oregano or ¼ teaspoon dried oregano**
- ½ **teaspoon pepper**
    Grated Parmesan cheese

1. In a Dutch oven, cook sausage and onion in oil until sausage is browned. Add garlic; cook 1 minute longer.

2. Stir in the beans, tomatoes, zucchini, broth, mushrooms, water, pesto, wine, vinegar, oregano and pepper. Bring to a boil. Reduce heat; simmer, uncovered, for 25-30 minutes or until vegetables are tender. Sprinkle with cheese.

Chicken Cacciatore Soup

My husband is Italian, and he gives this recipe an enthusiastic thumbs-up. Each spoonful is brimming with vegetables and tender pieces of chicken.

—**NANCY ROTH** ST. JOSEPH, IL

PREP: 25 MIN. • **COOK:** 25 MIN.
MAKES: 7 SERVINGS (ABOUT 2½ QUARTS)

- ½ **pound medium fresh mushrooms, quartered**
- 2 **medium leeks (white portion only), sliced**
- 2 **tablespoons olive oil**
- 3 **cans (14½ ounces each) reduced-sodium chicken broth**
- 3 **cups cubed cooked chicken**
- 1 **can (14½ ounces) diced tomatoes with basil, oregano and garlic, undrained**
- 1 **medium zucchini, quartered lengthwise and cut into ½-inch slices**
- 1 **each medium green, sweet red and yellow peppers, chopped**
- 1 **cup uncooked bow tie pasta**
- ½ **teaspoon dried thyme**
- ¼ **teaspoon pepper**
- ½ **cup shredded Parmesan cheese**
- ¼ **cup fresh basil leaves, thinly sliced**

1. In a Dutch oven, saute mushrooms and leeks in oil until tender. Stir in the broth, chicken, tomatoes, zucchini, peppers, pasta, thyme and pepper.
2. Bring to a boil. Reduce heat; simmer, uncovered, for 15-20 minutes or until pasta and vegetables are tender. Top each serving with cheese and basil.

A Dutch oven is a heavy covered pan. It's **very handy** because it can be used on the stovetop as well as the oven.

Quinoa Turkey Chili

This heart-healthy chili is not only delectable, it's also a powerhouse of vitamins and protein.

—**SHARON GILJUM** ARLINGTON, VA

PREP: 40 MIN. • **COOK:** 35 MIN.
MAKES: 9 SERVINGS (2¼ QUARTS)

- 1 **cup quinoa, rinsed**
- 3½ **cups water, divided**
- ½ **pound lean ground turkey**
- 1 **large sweet onion, chopped**
- 1 **medium sweet red pepper, chopped**
- 4 **garlic cloves, minced**
- 1 **tablespoon chili powder**
- 1 **tablespoon ground cumin**
- ½ **teaspoon ground cinnamon**
- 2 **cans (15 ounces each) black beans, rinsed and drained**
- 1 **can (28 ounces) crushed tomatoes**
- 1 **medium zucchini, chopped**
- 1 **chipotle pepper in adobo sauce, chopped**
- 1 **tablespoon adobo sauce**
- 1 **bay leaf**
- 1 **teaspoon dried oregano**
- ½ **teaspoon salt**
- ¼ **teaspoon pepper**
- 1 **cup frozen corn, thawed**
- ¼ **cup minced fresh cilantro**
  Peeled, cubed avocado and shredded cheese, optional

1. In a large saucepan, bring quinoa and 2 cups water to a boil. Reduce heat; cover and simmer for 12-15 minutes or until water is absorbed. Remove from the heat; fluff with a fork and set aside.
2. Meanwhile, in a large saucepan coated with cooking spray, cook the turkey, onion, red pepper and garlic over medium heat until meat is no longer pink and vegetables are tender; drain. Stir in the chili powder, cumin and cinnamon; cook 2 minutes longer.
3. Add the black beans, tomatoes, zucchini, chipotle pepper, adobo sauce, bay leaf, oregano, salt, pepper and remaining water. Bring to a boil. Reduce heat; cover and simmer for 30 minutes. Stir in corn and quinoa; heat through. Discard bay leaf; stir in cilantro. Top with avocado and cheese, if desired.

QUINOA TURKEY CHILI

> **My grandmother wrote a cookbook including a pie crust recipe. This soup features those buttery pastries.**
> —**KAREN LEMAY** PEARLAND, TX

CHICKEN POTPIE SOUP

Chicken Potpie Soup

PREP: 20 MIN. + CHILLING • **COOK:** 20 MIN.
MAKES: 6 SERVINGS

- 2 **cups all-purpose flour**
- 1¼ **teaspoons salt**
- ⅔ **cup shortening**
- 5 **to 6 tablespoons 2% milk**

SOUP

- 2 **tablespoons butter**
- 1 **cup cubed peeled potatoes**
- 1 **cup chopped sweet onion**
- 2 **celery ribs, chopped**
- 2 **medium carrots, chopped**
- ½ **cup all-purpose flour**
- ½ **teaspoon salt**
- ¼ **teaspoon pepper**

- 3 **cans (14½ ounces each) chicken broth**
- 2 **cups shredded cooked chicken**
- 1 **cup frozen petite peas**
- 1 **cup frozen corn**

1. In a large bowl, mix flour and salt; cut in shortening until crumbly. Gradually add milk, tossing with a fork until dough holds together when pressed. Shape into a disk; wrap in plastic wrap. Refrigerate for 30 minutes or overnight.

2. On a lightly floured surface, roll dough to ⅛-in. thickness. Using a floured 2½-in. heart-shaped or round cutter, cut 18 shapes. Place 1 in. apart on ungreased baking sheets. Bake at 425° for 8-11 minutes or until golden brown. Cool on a wire rack.

3. For soup, in a Dutch oven, heat butter over medium-high heat. Add the potatoes, onion, celery and carrots; cook and stir for 5-7 minutes or until onion is tender.

4. Stir in the flour, salt and pepper until blended; gradually whisk in broth. Bring to a boil, stirring occasionally. Reduce heat; simmer, uncovered, for 8-10 minutes or until potatoes are tender. Stir in remaining ingredients; heat through. Serve with pastries.

TURKEY MEATBALL SOUP

Turkey Meatball Soup

Every Italian-American family I know seems to have its own version of meatball soup, and it's no different for mine. I hope you enjoy our favorite way of preparing it.

—CHRISTIE LADD MECHANICSBURG, PA

PREP: 30 MIN. • **COOK:** 40 MIN.
MAKES: 6 SERVINGS

- 2 **egg whites, lightly beaten**
- ½ **cup seasoned bread crumbs**
- 1 **tablespoon grated Parmesan cheese**
- 4 **teaspoons Italian seasoning, divided**
- 1 **pound lean ground turkey**
- 3 **medium carrots, sliced**
- 3 **celery ribs, finely chopped**
- 1 **tablespoon olive oil**
- 4 **garlic cloves, minced**
- 3 **cans (14½ ounces each) reduced-sodium chicken broth**
- ¼ **teaspoon pepper**
- ½ **cup ditalini or other small pasta**

1. In a small bowl, combine the egg whites, bread crumbs, cheese and 2 teaspoons Italian seasoning. Crumble turkey over mixture and mix well. Shape into ¾-in. balls.

2. Place in a 15x10x 1-in. baking pan coated with cooking spray. Bake, uncovered, at 350° for 10-15 minutes or until no longer pink.

3. Meanwhile, in a Dutch oven, saute carrots and celery in oil for 5 minutes. Add garlic; cook 1 minute longer. Add the broth, pepper and remaining Italian seasoning. Bring to a boil. Reduce heat; cover and simmer for 15 minutes.

4. Stir in pasta; cook 10-12 minutes longer or until vegetables and pasta are tender. Add meatballs and heat through.

Turkey-Tarragon Noodle Soup

I think tarragon and turkey are a flavor match made in heaven—and this recipe proves it.

—CAROLYN KETCHUM WAKEFIELD, MA

START TO FINISH: 30 MIN.
MAKES: 6 SERVINGS

- 6 **cups chicken broth**
- 2 **medium carrots, thinly sliced**
- 1 **celery rib, thinly sliced**
- 2 **tablespoons lemon juice**
- 1 **bay leaf**
- ½ **teaspoon salt**
- ¼ **teaspoon pepper**
- 3 **cups uncooked medium egg noodles**
- 3 **cups coarsely chopped cooked turkey**
- 2 **tablespoons torn fresh tarragon leaves**
  Additional fresh tarragon leaves, optional

1. In a large saucepan, combine the first seven ingredients; bring to a boil. Reduce heat; cover and simmer for 8-10 minutes or until vegetables are tender.

2. Return to a boil; add noodles. Cook 5-6 minutes longer or until noodles are tender. Stir in turkey and tarragon; heat through. Discard bay leaf. If desired, top servings with additional tarragon leaves.

Stuffing Dumpling Soup

I've always loved turkey, dumplings and stuffing, so I combined them into a soup and added a punch of Creole flavor. If the spice is too much for you, try a dollop of sour cream to mellow it out.

—**RELINA SHIRLEY** RENO, NV

PREP: 20 MIN. • **COOK:** 25 MIN.
MAKES: 5 SERVINGS

- 1 cup sliced fresh mushrooms
- 1 medium onion, chopped
- 1 tablespoon olive oil
- 3 garlic cloves, minced
- 4 cups reduced-sodium chicken broth
- 1½ cups chopped fresh carrots
- 2 teaspoons Creole seasoning
- 2 eggs
- ½ cup all-purpose flour
- 2 cups cooked stuffing
- 2 cups cubed cooked turkey
- 1½ cups cut fresh green beans

1. In a Dutch oven, saute mushrooms and onion in oil until tender. Add garlic; cook 1 minute longer. Add the broth, carrots and Creole seasoning. Bring to a boil. Reduce heat; simmer, uncovered for 5-8 minutes or until carrots are tender.

2. Meanwhile, in a large bowl, whisk eggs and flour until smooth. Crumble stuffing over mixture; mix well. If necessary, add water, 1 teaspoon at a time, until mixture holds its shape.

3. Add the turkey and green beans to soup; return to a boil. Drop stuffing mixture by heaping tablespoonfuls onto simmering soup. Cover and simmer for 8-10 minutes or until a toothpick inserted into a dumpling comes out clean (do not lift the cover while simmering).

NOTE *The following spices may be substituted for 2 teaspoons Creole seasoning: ½ teaspoon each salt, garlic powder and paprika; and a pinch each of dried thyme, ground cumin and cayenne pepper.*

Turkey-White Bean Soup

Packed with nutrition, this marvelous soup will warm you up. For an extra-special touch, top each serving with shredded Parmesan cheese.

—**MARY RELYEA** CANASTOTA, NY

PREP: 20 MIN. • **COOK:** 40 MIN.
MAKES: 6 SERVINGS (2 QUARTS)

- 2 garlic cloves, minced
- 2 teaspoons olive oil
- ½ teaspoon dried rosemary, crushed
- ¼ teaspoon crushed red pepper flakes
- 1 can (28 ounces) whole tomatoes in puree, cut up
- 1 can (14½ ounces) reduced-sodium chicken broth
- 2 cups shredded carrots
- 2 cans (15 ounces each) white kidney or cannellini beans, rinsed and drained
- 1 package (6 ounces) fresh baby spinach, chopped
- 1½ cups cubed cooked turkey breast Shredded Parmesan cheese, optional

1. In a large saucepan over medium heat, cook garlic in oil for 1 minute. Add rosemary and pepper flakes; cook 1 minute longer.

2. Stir in the tomatoes, broth and carrots. Bring to a boil. Reduce heat; cover and simmer for 15 minutes. Stir in the beans, spinach and turkey; return to a boil. Reduce heat; cover and simmer 10 minutes longer. Serve with cheese if desired.

TURKEY-WHITE BEAN SOUP

CURRIED CHICKEN SOUP

Curried Chicken Soup

This was a longtime favorite recipe that my grandmother used to make. I've added my own special touches to it, such as the chickpeas, coconut milk and the fresh cilantro.

—**DEANNA HINDENACH** PAW PAW, MI

PREP: 25 MIN. • **COOK:** 45 MIN.
MAKES: 8 SERVINGS

- 4 teaspoons curry powder
- ½ teaspoon salt
- ½ teaspoon pepper
- ½ teaspoon cayenne pepper
- 1 pound boneless skinless chicken breasts, cut into 1-inch cubes
- 3 medium carrots, chopped
- 1 medium sweet red pepper, chopped
- 1 small onion, chopped
- 2 tablespoons olive oil
- 1 garlic clove, minced
- 1 can (15 ounces) garbanzo beans or chickpeas, rinsed and drained
- 1 can (14½ ounces) chicken broth
- 1 can (14½ ounces) diced tomatoes, drained
- 1 cup water
- 1 can (13.66 ounces) coconut milk
- ¾ cup minced fresh cilantro

1. In a large resealable plastic bag, combine the curry, salt, pepper and cayenne. Add chicken, a few pieces at a time, and shake to coat.

2. In a large saucepan over medium heat, cook the chicken, carrots, red pepper and onion in oil for 4 minutes. Add garlic; cook 1-2 minutes longer or until chicken is browned and vegetables are tender; drain.

3. Stir in the garbanzo beans, broth, tomatoes and water. Bring to a boil. Reduce heat; cover and simmer for 30 minutes. Stir in coconut milk; heat through. Garnish servings with cilantro.

Thanksgiving's Not Over Yet Enchilada Soup

Pumpkin adds a unique richness to this warm soup. You certainly can include Thanksgiving leftovers, but it's a good recipe to turn to any time you have extra turkey.

—**DENISE POUNDS** HUTCHINSON, KS

PREP: 20 MIN. • **COOK:** 20 MIN.
MAKES: 8 SERVINGS (3 QUARTS)

- 1 large sweet red pepper, finely chopped
- 1 medium onion, chopped
- 1 celery rib, chopped
- 1 tablespoon olive oil
- 2 cans (14½ ounces each) reduced-sodium chicken broth
- 1 can (28 ounces) green enchilada sauce
- 1 can (15 ounces) solid-pack pumpkin
- 1½ cups frozen corn
- 2 cans (4 ounces each) chopped green chilies
- 2 tablespoons ranch salad dressing mix
- 2 cups cubed cooked turkey
  Optional toppings: crumbled queso fresco, shredded cheddar cheese, crushed tortilla chips, cubed avocado and minced fresh cilantro

In a Dutch oven, saute the red pepper, onion and celery in oil until crisp-tender. Add the broth, enchilada sauce, pumpkin, corn, chilies and dressing mix. Bring to a boil. Reduce heat; cover and simmer for 10-12 minutes or until vegetables are tender. Stir in turkey and heat through. Garnish servings with toppings of your choice.

NEW ORLEANS GUMBO

Italian Wedding Soup

You don't have to be Italian to love this easy to make soup! It's always a hit when I serve it.

—**MARY SHEETZ** CARMEL, IN

PREP: 30 MIN. • **COOK:** 40 MIN.
MAKES: 9 SERVINGS (2¼ QUARTS)

- 2 eggs, lightly beaten
- ½ cup dry bread crumbs
- ¼ cup minced fresh parsley
- 2 tablespoons grated Parmesan cheese
- 1 tablespoon raisins, finely chopped
- 3 garlic cloves, minced
- ¼ teaspoon crushed red pepper flakes
- ½ pound lean ground beef (90% lean)
- ½ pound bulk spicy pork sausage
- 2 cartons (32 ounces each) reduced-sodium chicken broth
- ½ teaspoon pepper
- 1½ cups cubed rotisserie chicken
- ⅔ cup uncooked acini di pepe pasta
- ½ cup fresh baby spinach, cut into thin strips
  Shredded Parmesan cheese, optional

1. In a large bowl, combine the first seven ingredients. Crumble beef and sausage over mixture and mix well. Shape into ½-in. balls.
2. In a Dutch oven, brown meatballs in small batches; drain. Add the broth and pepper; bring to a boil. Reduce heat; simmer, uncovered, for 10 minutes. Stir in chicken and pasta; cook 5-7 minutes longer or until pasta is tender. Stir in spinach; cook until wilted. Sprinkle with shredded Parmesan cheese if desired.

New Orleans Gumbo

I've been making this gumbo for at least 30 years. I'm originally from New Orleans, and I think it's a nice taste of the Vieux Carre (French Quarter). Everyone who tastes this gumbo wants the recipe. It's an old standby for members of my family, who request it frequently.

—**DOLORES BRIDGES** DANVILLE, KY

PREP: 25 MIN. • **COOK:** 20 MIN.
MAKES: 8 SERVINGS

- 2 cups chicken broth
- 1 cup uncooked converted rice
- 2 celery ribs, chopped
- 1 medium onion, chopped
- 2 garlic cloves, minced
- 1 can (28 ounces) diced tomatoes, undrained
- 1 pound boneless skinless chicken breasts, cut into ½-inch cubes
- ½ pound smoked kielbasa or Polish sausage, cut into ½-inch slices
- 1 teaspoon dried thyme
- 1 teaspoon pepper
- 2 bay leaves
- ¼ teaspoon cayenne pepper
- 3 tablespoons all-purpose flour
- ¼ cup cold water
- 1 pound uncooked medium shrimp, peeled and deveined
- 1 large green pepper, chopped
- ¼ cup minced fresh parsley

1. In a large saucepan, bring broth to a boil. Stir in the rice, celery, onion and garlic. Reduce heat; cover and simmer for 20 minutes.
2. Meanwhile, in a Dutch oven, combine the tomatoes, chicken, kielbasa, thyme, pepper, bay leaves and cayenne. Bring to a boil. Reduce heat; cover and simmer for 10 minutes.
3. Combine flour and water until smooth; gradually stir into chicken mixture. Stir in shrimp and green pepper. Cook, uncovered, over medium heat for 4-6 minutes or until shrimp turn pink and gumbo is thickened. Discard bay leaves.
4. Remove rice from the heat and let stand for 5 minutes; stir in parsley. Serve with gumbo.

(5) INGREDIENTS
Dandelion Soup

Welcome spring with this change-of-pace soup! I guarantee you'll have compliments cropping up like weeds after dishing it out to family and friends.
—**MARY ELLEN DYCUS** LELAND, MS

START TO FINISH: 25 MIN.
MAKES: 10-12 SERVINGS

- 1 package (6.9 ounces) chicken-flavored rice mix
- 3 cans (10¾ ounces each) condensed cream of chicken soup, undiluted
- 5 cups water
- 2 cups cubed cooked chicken
- 4 cups torn dandelion greens

Prepare rice according to package directions; set aside. In a large saucepan or Dutch oven over medium heat, combine soup and water. Add rice and chicken; heat through. Add dandelion greens; cook until tender, about 6-8 minutes.

(5) INGREDIENTS
Quick Ravioli & Spinach Soup

I love my Italian-American traditions but I didn't have time to make a classic wedding soup, which is when I created this shortcut version with ravioli.
—**CYNTHIA BENT** NEWARK, DE

START TO FINISH: 25 MIN.
MAKES: 6 SERVINGS

- 2 cartons (32 ounces each) chicken broth
- ¼ teaspoon onion powder
  Dash pepper
- 1 package (9 ounces) refrigerated small cheese ravioli
- 4 cups coarsely chopped fresh spinach (about 4 ounces)
- 3 cups shredded cooked chicken
  Grated Parmesan cheese, optional

In a large saucepan, combine the broth, onion powder and pepper; bring to a boil. Add ravioli; cook, uncovered, for 7-10 minutes or until tender. Add spinach and chicken during the last 3 minutes of cooking. If desired, serve with cheese.

COCONUT CURRY CHICKEN SOUP

Coconut Curry Chicken Soup

Similar to a Vietnamese pho rice noodle soup, this red curry vermicelli noodle soup packs big taste and a bit of heat. The crisp raw vegetables help cool things down.
—**MONNIE NORASING** MANSFIELD, TX

PREP: 20 MIN. • **COOK:** 35 MIN.
MAKES: 6 SERVINGS

- 2 cans (13.66 ounces each) coconut milk
- ⅓ to ½ cup red curry paste
- 1 package (8.8 ounces) thin rice noodles
- 2 cans (14½ ounces each) chicken broth
- ¼ cup packed brown sugar
- 2 tablespoons fish sauce or soy sauce
- ¾ teaspoon garlic salt
- 3 cups shredded rotisserie chicken
- 1½ cups shredded cabbage
- 1½ cups shredded carrots
- ¾ cup bean sprouts
  Fresh basil and cilantro leaves

1. In a Dutch oven, bring coconut milk to a boil. Cook, uncovered, 10-12 minutes or until liquid is reduced to 3 cups. Stir in curry paste until dissolved.
2. Meanwhile, prepare noodles according to package directions.
3. Add broth, brown sugar, fish sauce and garlic salt to curry mixture; return to a boil. Reduce heat; simmer, uncovered, 10 minutes, stirring occasionally. Stir in chicken; heat through.
4. Drain noodles; divide among six large soup bowls. Ladle soup over noodles; top servings with vegetables, basil and cilantro.
NOTE *This recipe was tested with Thai Kitchen Red Curry Paste.*

Skinny Turkey-Vegetable Soup

If you need a pick-me-up meal, look no further. This soup will fill you up without being overwhelming.

—**CHARLOTTE WELCH** UTICA, NY

PREP: 30 MIN. • **COOK:** 35 MIN.
MAKES: 6 SERVINGS (2¼ QUARTS)

- 2 **medium onions, chopped**
- 2 **medium carrots, halved and thinly sliced**
- 2 **celery ribs, chopped**
- ½ **cup chopped sweet red pepper**
- 1 **tablespoon olive oil**
- 3 **garlic cloves, minced**
- 4 **cups water**
- 1 **can (10 ounces) diced tomatoes and green chilies, undrained**
- ½ **cup frozen peas**
- 1 **bay leaf**
- 4 **teaspoons sodium-free chicken bouillon granules**
- ½ **teaspoon dried basil**
- ½ **teaspoon dried thyme**
- ¼ **teaspoon ground cumin**
- ¼ **teaspoon pepper**
- ¼ **to ½ teaspoon hot pepper sauce, optional**
- ½ **cup uncooked whole wheat orzo pasta**
- 2 **cups cubed cooked turkey breast**
- 1 **tablespoon minced fresh cilantro**

1. In a large saucepan, saute the onions, carrots, celery and red pepper in oil until tender. Add garlic; cook 2 minutes longer. Stir in the water, tomatoes, peas, bay leaf, bouillon, basil, thyme, cumin, pepper and pepper sauce if desired. Bring to a boil. Reduce heat; simmer, uncovered, for 15 minutes.

2. Meanwhile, cook orzo according to package directions; drain. Stir orzo and turkey into soup; heat through. Discard bay leaf. Sprinkle with fresh cilantro.

Chicken Chili Chowder

One chilly afternoon, I wanted a homemade soup but had less than an hour to prepare it. I came up with this chowder using ingredients I had on hand, and everyone thought it hit the spot.

—**JENNA REMPE** LINCOLN, NE

PREP: 15 MIN. • **COOK:** 25 MIN.
MAKES: 6 SERVINGS (2 QUARTS)

- 1 **medium onion, chopped**
- 2 **teaspoons canola oil**
- 5 **medium red potatoes, cubed**
- 1 **can (14½ ounces) chicken broth**
- 1 **can (10¾ ounces) condensed cream of chicken soup, undiluted**
- ½ **cup salsa verde**
- 1 **teaspoon chili powder**
- ½ **teaspoon garlic powder**
- ½ **teaspoon ground cumin**
- ½ **teaspoon pepper**
- ¼ **teaspoon salt**
- 2 **cups cubed cooked chicken breast**
- 1 **can (15½ ounces) great northern beans, rinsed and drained**
- 1 **can (14¾ ounces) cream-style corn**
  Shredded cheddar cheese and sour cream, optional

Saute onion in oil in a large saucepan until tender. Add potatoes, broth, soup, salsa and seasonings. Bring to a boil. Reduce heat; cover and simmer for 15-20 minutes or until potatoes are tender. Stir in the chicken, beans and corn; heat through. Serve with cheese and sour cream if desired.

CHICKEN CHILI CHOWDER

Pork, Ham & Sausage

36   42   40

What better way to hearty up a soup than with a little **bacon, sausage and ham?** Add these ingredients to soups and stews and you have bowlfuls of deliciousness the whole **family will love.** You might want to double the recipes from the start, however, because these appealing **stick-to-your-ribs favorites** will disappear in a flash.

HOT AND SOUR SOUP

Hot and Sour Soup

After trying several recipes in hopes of replicating a soup I liked at a restaurant, I came up with my own. I must say it is on par with what you'll find when dining out. Use regular or hot chili sauce, depending on your spice tolerance.

—**VERA LEITOW** MANCELONA, MI

PREP: 20 MIN. • **COOK:** 25 MIN.
MAKES: 6 SERVINGS (ABOUT 2 QUARTS)

- ¾ **pound pork tenderloin, cut into 1½-inch x ¼-inch strips**
- 1 **tablespoon olive oil**
- ½ **pound sliced fresh mushrooms**
- 6 **cups chicken broth**
- ¼ **cup soy sauce**
- 2 **tablespoons chili garlic sauce**
- ¾ **teaspoon pepper**
- 1 **package (14 ounces) extra-firm tofu, drained and cut into ¼-inch cubes**
- 1 **can (8 ounces) bamboo shoots, drained**
- 1 **can (8 ounces) sliced water chestnuts, drained**
- ½ **cup white vinegar**
- ⅓ **cup cornstarch**
- ⅓ **cup cold water**
- 2 **teaspoons sesame oil**
  Finely chopped green onions

1. In a Dutch oven, brown pork in oil until no longer pink; remove meat and keep warm. Add mushrooms; saute until tender. Set aside and keep warm.
2. Add the broth, soy sauce, chili garlic sauce and pepper to the pan. Bring to a boil. Reduce heat; cover and simmer for 10 minutes. Return the meat and mushrooms to the pan. Stir in the tofu, bamboo shoots, water chestnuts and vinegar. Simmer, uncovered, for 10 minutes.
3. In a small bowl, combine cornstarch and water until smooth; gradually stir into soup. Bring to a boil; cook and stir for 2 minutes or until thickened. Remove from the heat; stir in sesame oil. Garnish servings with onions.

Black-Eyed Pea Soup

Green chilies give this dish a little Southwestern flair. I've also used ground beef instead of pork with good results.

—**MARY LOU CHERNIK** TAOS, NM

PREP: 5 MIN. • **COOK:** 55 MIN.
MAKES: 12 SERVINGS (ABOUT 3 QUARTS)

- 1½ **pounds ground pork**
- 1 **large onion, chopped**
- 2 **garlic cloves, minced**
- 3 **cans (15½ ounces each) black-eyed peas, rinsed and drained**
- 2 **cups water**
- 1 **can (14½ ounces) stewed tomatoes**
- 1 **can (10 ounces) diced tomatoes and green chilies**
- 1 **can (4 ounces) chopped green chilies**
- 1 **tablespoon beef bouillon granules**
- 1 **tablespoon molasses**
- 1 **teaspoon Worcestershire sauce**
- ½ **teaspoon salt**
- ¼ **teaspoon pepper**
- ¼ **teaspoon ground cumin**

In a large soup kettle or Dutch oven, cook the pork, onion and garlic over medium heat until meat is no longer pink; drain. Stir in the remaining ingredients; bring to a boil. Reduce heat; cover and simmer for 45 minutes.

Echo Valley Bean Soup

I came up with this recipe after sampling some excellent bean soup at a sandwich shop in a neighboring town.

—**PATRICIA CRANDALL** INCHELIUM, WA

START TO FINISH: 30 MIN.
MAKES: 6 SERVINGS

- 10 **bacon strips, diced**
- 1 **medium onion, diced**
- 2 **garlic cloves, minced**
- 1 **can (14½ ounces) stewed tomatoes**
- 2 **cans (15 ounces each) pork and beans**
- 2 **cans (14½ ounces each) beef broth**

1. In a saucepan, cook bacon until crisp. Set bacon aside; drain grease from pan, reserving 1-2 tablespoons drippings. Saute the onion and garlic in drippings until tender.
2. Meanwhile, in a blender, process tomatoes until smooth. Add to the onion mixture. Stir in pork and beans and broth. Bring to a boil. Reduce heat; simmer, uncovered, for 15 minutes or until heated through. Stir in bacon.

Sausage Lentil Soup

I first tried this wonderful soup at a friend's house. Now it's my favorite, especially when we start to head into autumn or winter.

—**CATHERINE ROWE** BERTHOUD, CO

PREP: 10 MIN. • **COOK:** 1 HOUR
MAKES: 6 SERVINGS

- ½ **pound bulk Italian sausage**
- 1 **large onion, finely chopped**
- 1 **small green pepper, finely chopped**
- 1 **small carrots, finely chopped**
- 1 **large garlic clove, finely minced**
- 1 **bay leaf**
- 2 **cans (14½ ounces each) chicken broth**
- 1 **can (14½ ounces) diced tomatoes, undrained**
- 1 **cup water**
- ¾ **cup dried lentils, rinsed**
- ¼ **cup country-style or regular Dijon mustard**

In a Dutch oven, cook sausage over medium heat until no longer pink. Drain fat and crumble sausage; return to Dutch oven along with remaining ingredients except mustard. Simmer, covered, 1 hour or until lentils and vegetables are tender. Stir in mustard. Discard bay leaf before serving.

Andouille-Shrimp Cream Soup

PREP: 20 MIN. • **COOK:** 30 MIN.
MAKES: 7 SERVINGS

- ½ **pound fully cooked andouille sausage links, thinly sliced**
- 1 **medium onion, chopped**
- 2 **celery ribs, thinly sliced**
- 1 **medium sweet red pepper, chopped**
- 1 **medium green pepper, chopped**
- 1 **jalapeno pepper, seeded and chopped**
- ¼ **cup butter, cubed**
- 3 **garlic cloves, minced**
- 2 **cups fresh or frozen corn, thawed**
- 4 **plum tomatoes, chopped**
- 1 **cup vegetable broth**
- 2 **tablespoons minced fresh thyme or 2 teaspoons dried thyme**
- 1 **teaspoon chili powder**
- ½ **teaspoon salt**
- ½ **teaspoon pepper**
- ¼ **to ½ teaspoon cayenne pepper**
- 1 **pound uncooked medium shrimp, peeled and deveined**
- 1 **cup heavy whipping cream**

1. In a large skillet, saute the first six ingredients in butter until vegetables are tender. Add garlic; cook 1 minute longer. Add the corn, tomatoes, broth, thyme, chili powder, salt, pepper and cayenne. Bring to a boil. Reduce heat; simmer, uncovered, for 10 minutes.

2. Stir in shrimp and cream. Bring to a gentle boil. Simmer, uncovered, for 8-10 minutes or until shrimp turn pink.

NOTE *Wear disposable gloves when cutting hot peppers; the oils can burn skin. Avoid touching your face.*

Inspired by southern Louisiana corn stew, this recipe beautifully blends andouille sausage with the shrimp and subtle spices.

—**JUDY ARMSTRONG** PRAIRIEVILLE, LA

ANDOUILLE-SHRIMP CREAM SOUP

Winter Country Soup

My soup will warm your family up on the chilliest nights! Featuring smoked sausage, beans and other vegetables, it's a hearty way to start a meal or a tasty lunch all by itself.

—JEANNETTE SABO LEXINGTON PARK, MD

PREP: 15 MIN. • **COOK:** 40 MIN.
MAKES: 12 SERVINGS (3 QUARTS)

- 1 package (14 ounces) smoked sausage, cut into ¼-inch slices
- 1 large sweet red pepper, cut into ½-inch pieces
- 8 shallots, chopped
- 1 tablespoon butter
- 8 cups chopped fresh kale
- 8 cups vegetable broth
- 3 cups frozen corn
- 1 can (15½ ounces) great northern beans, rinsed and drained
- ½ teaspoon cayenne pepper
- ¼ teaspoon pepper
- ¾ cup uncooked orzo pasta

1. In a Dutch oven, saute the sausage, red pepper and shallots in butter until vegetables are tender.
2. Add kale; cover and cook for 2-3 minutes or until kale is wilted. Stir in the broth, corn, beans, cayenne and pepper. Bring to a boil. Reduce heat; simmer, uncovered, for 20 minutes. Return to a boil. Stir in orzo. Cook 8-10 minutes longer or until the pasta is tender.

Creamy Ham & Corn Soup

My quick and easy soup really hits the spot on a cold winter night. (And yes, we do occasionally have those in Arizona!)

—AUDREY THIBODEAU GILBERT, AZ

START TO FINISH: 30 MIN.
MAKES: 7 SERVINGS

- 2 cans (14½ ounces each) chicken broth
- 2 cups fresh or frozen corn
- 1 cup half-and-half cream
- ⅓ cup chopped onion
- ⅓ cup chopped sweet red pepper
- ¼ cup plus 3 tablespoons all-purpose flour
- ½ cup cold water
- ½ teaspoon salt
- ¼ teaspoon pepper
- 1 cup diced fully cooked ham
  Snipped fresh dill, optional

1. Combine the broth, corn, cream, onion and red pepper in a large saucepan. Bring to a boil. Combine the flour, water, salt and pepper until smooth; gradually stir into pan. Bring to a boil; cook and stir for 2 minutes or until thickened. Stir in ham.
2. Reduce heat; cover and simmer for 10-15 minutes or until vegetables are tender. Garnish servings with dill if desired.

Add a garnish to your soup to make the presentation fun. Croutons, snipped fresh dill, a dollop of sour cream, grated cheese—**the possibilities are endless.**

UPSTATE MINESTRONE

French Market Soup

A friend gave me this recipe. I think it's best the next day, so I recommend preparing it the day before serving. Leftovers also freeze well.

—TERRI LOWE LUMBERTON, TX

PREP: 20 MIN. + SOAKING
COOK: 4½ HOURS
MAKES: 12 SERVINGS (4½ QUARTS)

- 3 cups assorted dried beans for soup
- 2 smoked ham hocks
- 12 cups water
- 1½ teaspoons salt
- ½ teaspoon pepper
- 1 can (28 ounces) crushed tomatoes, undrained
- 2 medium onions, chopped
- ¼ to ⅓ cup lemon juice
- 2 garlic cloves, minced
- ½ teaspoon chili powder
- 1 pound smoked kielbasa, chopped
- 1½ cups cubed cooked chicken
- ½ cup dry red wine or chicken broth
- ½ cup minced fresh parsley

1. Sort beans and rinse in cold water. Place beans in a Dutch oven; add water to cover by 2 in. Bring to a boil; boil for 2 minutes. Remove from the heat; cover and let beans stand for 1-4 hours or until softened.
2. Drain and rinse beans, discarding liquid; return beans to the pan. Add the ham hocks, water, salt and pepper; bring to a boil. Reduce heat; cover and simmer for 3 hours or until the beans are tender.
3. Remove ham hocks; set aside until cool enough to handle. Add tomatoes, onions, lemon juice, garlic and chili powder to the beans. Simmer 1 hour longer.
4. Remove ham from bones and cut into cubes; discard bones. Return ham to soup. Stir in the kielbasa, chicken, wine and parsley. Simmer soup for 30-40 minutes or until heated through and as thick as desired.
NOTE *This recipe was tested with Bob's Red Mill 13-Bean Soup Mix.*

Upstate Minestrone

If you love vegetables, you'll find this minestrone especially satisfying. Keep the recipe in mind when you have a bounty of fresh garden produce.

—YVONNE KRANTZ MOUNT UPTON, NY

PREP: 25 MIN. • **COOK:** 1 HOUR 20 MIN.
MAKES: 8 SERVINGS

- 1 pound Italian sausage links, cut into ½-inch slices
- 1 tablespoon olive oil
- 1 cup finely chopped onion
- 1 cup sliced fresh carrots
- 1 garlic clove, finely minced
- 1 teaspoon dried basil
- 2 cups shredded cabbage
- 2 small zucchini, sliced
- 2 cans (10½ ounces each) condensed beef broth, undiluted, or 3 beef bouillon cubes plus 1½ cups hot water
- 1 can (14½ ounces) diced tomatoes, undrained
- 1 teaspoon salt
- ¼ teaspoon pepper
- 1 can (15½ ounces) great northern beans, rinsed and drained
  Minced fresh parsley

1. In a Dutch oven, brown sausage in oil. Add the onion, carrots, garlic and basil; cook for 5 minutes. Stir in the cabbage, zucchini, broth, tomatoes, salt and pepper.
2. Bring to a boil. Reduce heat; cover and simmer for 1 hour. Add beans; cook 20 minutes longer. Garnish with parsley.

Root Vegetable Soup with Sausage

After trying a similar soup at a restaurant, I went home and made it for myself. To my surprise, it came out even better than the original! This soup actually won top honors in our town's annual cook-off.

—DONNA CLASS KEYSER, WV

PREP: 30 MIN. • **COOK:** 45 MIN.
MAKES: 20 SERVINGS (1 CUP EACH)

- ½ pound bulk Italian sausage
- 1 medium butternut squash (about 3 pounds), peeled and cubed
- 4 large potatoes, peeled and cubed
- 3 large sweet potatoes, peeled and cubed
- 1 large rutabaga, peeled and cubed
- 1 pound fresh baby carrots
- 1 medium turnip, peeled and diced
- 10 cups water
- 2 cans (14½ ounces each) vegetable broth
- 2 tablespoons sugar
- 1½ teaspoons salt
- 1 teaspoon ground ginger
- ⅛ teaspoon pepper
- ¼ cup heavy whipping cream

1. Crumble sausage into a stockpot. Cook over medium heat until no longer pink; drain.

2. Stir in the vegetables, water, broth, sugar and seasonings; bring to a boil. Reduce heat; cover and simmer for 35-40 minutes or until vegetables are tender. Cool slightly.

3. In a blender, process soup in batches until smooth. Return to the pan; whisk in cream. Heat through (do not boil).

Cassoulet for the Gang

Wine lends a warm background taste to this take on traditional French stew. The recipe feeds 10, so it's great when you're expecting guests.

—LYNN STEIN JOSEPH, OR

PREP: 25 MIN. • **COOK:** 40 MIN.
MAKES: 10 SERVINGS (4 QUARTS)

- 1 pork tenderloin (1 pound), cut into ½-inch pieces
- 1 pound smoked turkey kielbasa, cut into ½-inch pieces
- 1 tablespoon olive oil
- 3 medium carrots, chopped
- 1 large onion, cut into wedges
- 4 garlic cloves, minced
- 2 cans (14½ ounces each) no-salt-added stewed tomatoes, cut up
- 1 can (14½ ounces) reduced-sodium chicken broth
- 3 teaspoons herbes de Provence
- 1½ teaspoons garlic powder
- 1½ teaspoons dried basil
- ½ teaspoon dried oregano
- ¼ teaspoon pepper
- 4 cans (15½ ounces each) great northern beans, rinsed and drained, divided
- ¾ cup white wine or additional chicken broth, divided

1. In a Dutch oven coated with cooking spray, saute the pork and kielbasa in oil until lightly browned; drain. Add carrots and onion; saute 4 minutes longer. Add garlic; cook for 1 minute longer. Stir in the tomatoes, broth and seasonings. Bring to a boil. Reduce heat; cover and simmer for 10 minutes.

2. Place one can of beans in a food processor; add ¼ cup wine or broth. Cover and process until pureed. Stir into meat mixture. Stir in remaining beans and wine or broth. Bring to a boil. Reduce heat; simmer, uncovered, for 8-10 minutes or until meat and vegetables are tender.

NOTE *Look for herbes de Provence in the spice aisle.*

CASSOULET FOR THE GANG

SWISS POTATO SOUP

Italian Wedding Soup with Meatballs

I first simmered up a batch of this soup when it was featured in our local newspaper. Instead of ground pork you can substitute chicken sausage, rolled up into little balls, for the meatballs.
—**AMY MCGOWEN** JUPITER, FL

PREP: 30 MIN. + FREEZING • **COOK:** 40 MIN.
MAKES: 7 SERVINGS

- 1 **egg white**
- ¼ **cup panko (Japanese) bread crumbs**
- 1 **teaspoon Italian seasoning**
- ½ **pound ground pork**
- 2 **medium carrots, chopped**
- 2 **celery ribs, chopped**
- 1 **medium parsnip, peeled and chopped**
- 1 **small onion, finely chopped**
- 2 **tablespoons olive oil**
- 6 **cups reduced-sodium chicken broth**
- 3 **teaspoons herbes de Provence**
- ½ **teaspoon crushed red pepper flakes**
- ½ **teaspoon pepper**
- 1 **cup uncooked orzo pasta**
- 1 **package (6 ounces) fresh baby spinach**
- ¼ **cup shredded Parmesan cheese**
- ¼ **cup minced fresh parsley**

1. In a large bowl, combine the egg white, bread crumbs and Italian seasoning. Crumble pork over mixture and mix well. Shape into ¾-in. balls.
2. Place meatballs on a greased rack in a foil-lined 15x10x1-in. baking pan. Bake at 350° for 15-18 minutes or until a thermometer reads 160°.
3. Meanwhile, in a Dutch oven, saute the carrots, celery, parsnip and onion in oil until tender. Stir in the broth, herbes de Provence, pepper flakes and pepper.
4. Drain meatballs on paper towels. Bring soup to a boil; add meatballs. Reduce heat; simmer, uncovered, for 30 minutes. Cool. Transfer to freezer containers. Soup may be frozen for up to 3 months.
NOTE *Look for herbes de Provence in the spice aisle.*

Swiss Potato Soup

You have a few options when it comes to fixing this soup. It can also be made in the microwave or started in a slow cooker in the morning.
—**KRISTA MUSSER** ORRVILLE, OH

START TO FINISH: 30 MIN.
MAKES: 4 SERVINGS

- 5 **bacon strips, diced**
- 1 **medium onion, chopped**
- 2 **cups water**
- 4 **medium potatoes, peeled and cubed**
- 1½ **teaspoons salt**
- ⅛ **teaspoon pepper**
- ⅓ **cup all-purpose flour**
- 2 **cups 2% milk**
- 1 **cup (4 ounces) shredded Swiss cheese**

1. In a large saucepan, cook bacon until crisp; remove to paper towels with a slotted spoon. Drain, reserving 1 tablespoon drippings.
2. Saute onion in drippings until tender. Add water, potatoes, salt and pepper. Bring to a boil. Reduce heat; simmer, uncovered, for 12 minutes or until potatoes are tender.
3. Combine flour and milk until smooth; gradually stir in potato mixture. Bring to a boil; cook and stir for 2 minutes or until thickened and bubbly. Remove from the heat; stir in cheese until melted. Sprinkle with bacon.

ITALIAN WEDDING SOUP WITH MEATBALLS

Chili Verde

This is one of my family's favorite recipes. We enjoy it any time of year, but it's especially good with fresh peppers from the garden.

—SHERRIE SCETTRINI SALINAS, CA

PREP: 15 MIN. • **COOK:** 1¾ HOURS
MAKES: 8 SERVINGS

- 4 **tablespoons canola oil, divided**
- 4 **pounds boneless pork, cut into ¾-inch cubes**
- ¼ **cup all-purpose flour**
- 1 **can (4 ounces) chopped green chilies**
- ½ **teaspoon ground cumin**
- ¼ **teaspoon salt**
- ¼ **teaspoon pepper**
- 3 **garlic cloves, minced**
- ½ **cup minced fresh cilantro**
- ½ **to 1 cup salsa**
- 1 **can (14½ ounces) chicken broth**
  Flour tortillas, warmed

1. In a Dutch oven, heat 1 tablespoon oil over medium-high. Add 1 pound of pork; cook and stir until lightly browned. Remove and set aside. Repeat with remaining meat, adding more oil as needed. Return all of the meat to Dutch oven.
2. Sprinkle flour over meat; mix well. Add the chilies, cumin, salt, pepper, garlic, cilantro, salsa and broth. Cover and simmer until pork is tender and chili reaches the desired consistency, about 1½ hours. Serve with warmed tortillas.

FARMHOUSE HAM CHOWDER

Leftover ham and veggies add substance to this hearty chowder, but ranch dressing is the recipe's zesty secret. Stirring in the smoked Gouda adds a bit of cheesy goodness.

—LISA RENSHAW KANSAS CITY, MO

Farmhouse Ham Chowder

PREP: 10 MIN. • **COOK:** 30 MIN.
MAKES: 8 SERVINGS (2 QUARTS)

- ½ **cup finely chopped onion**
- ½ **cup finely chopped celery**
- ½ **cup chopped sweet red pepper**
- 2 **tablespoons butter**
- ¼ **cup all-purpose flour**
- 1 **envelope ranch salad dressing mix**
- 4¼ **cups milk**
- 2 **cups frozen cubed hash brown potatoes, thawed**
- 2 **cups frozen corn, thawed**
- 2 **cups cubed fully cooked ham**
- 1 **teaspoon minced fresh thyme or ¼ teaspoon dried thyme**
- ½ **cup shredded smoked Gouda cheese**

1. In a large saucepan, saute the onion, celery and red pepper in butter until crisp-tender. Stir in flour and dressing mix until blended; gradually stir in milk. Bring to a boil; cook and stir for 2 minutes or until thickened.
2. Add the potatoes, corn, ham and thyme. Bring to a boil. Reduce heat; simmer, uncovered, for 8-10 minutes to allow flavors to blend. Stir in cheese until blended.

Asian Pork and Noodle Soup

This soup can be made in a flash and features flavor from ginger, sesame, soy sauce and green onions. Cantonese bean thread noodles, also called cellophane noodles, are typically soaked in hot water for 10-15 minutes, then rinsed and used in soups and stir-fries.

—**JEAN HINES** GOODYEAR, AZ

START TO FINISH: 30 MIN.
MAKES: 6 SERVINGS

- 2 **ounces uncooked bean thread noodles**
- 2 **medium carrots, cut into ¼-inch diagonal slices**
- 1 **cup coarsely chopped bok choy**
- 1 **tablespoon sesame oil**
- 1 **tablespoon minced fresh gingerroot**
- 3½ **cups reduced-sodium chicken broth**
- 1 **cup water**
- 1 **tablespoon reduced-sodium soy sauce**
- ¼ **teaspoon coarsely ground pepper**
- ¾ **cup cubed cooked pork tenderloin**
- 3 **green onions, thinly sliced diagonally**

Soak noodles according to package directions. Meanwhile, in a large saucepan, saute carrots and bok choy in oil until tender. Add ginger; cook 1 minute longer. Stir in the broth, water, soy sauce, pepper and noodles. Bring to a boil. Reduce heat; simmer until noodles are tender. Stir in pork and green onions; heat through.

Ham & Corn Chowder

Generous amounts of corn, ham and potato turn this into a fast favorite. No one will know it came together in 25 minutes, especially if you add the pretty garnishes on top.

—**MARION ST. JEAN** HOMOSASSA, FL

START TO FINISH: 25 MIN.
MAKES: 6 SERVINGS

- 1 **can (10¾ ounces) reduced-fat reduced-sodium condensed cream of celery soup, undiluted**
- 1½ **cups fat-free milk**
- 1 **can (15¼ ounces) whole kernel corn, drained**
- 1 **can (14¾ ounces) cream-style corn**
- ½ **cup cubed fully cooked ham**
- 2 **tablespoons dried minced onion**
- 2 **tablespoons minced fresh parsley**
- 1 **can (14½ ounces) diced potatoes, drained**
   Sour cream, shredded cheddar cheese and/or paprika, optional

In a large saucepan, combine soup and milk. Heat through, stirring frequently. Stir in the corn, ham, onion and parsley. Bring to a boil. Reduce heat; cover and simmer for 5 minutes. Stir in potatoes; heat through. Garnish with sour cream, cheese and/or paprika if desired.

ASIAN PORK AND NOODLE SOUP

Creamy Cauliflower Soup with Artichoke Hearts & Bacon

When I had surgery, my oldest son, a chef, came to cook my meals. He ended up making a simple cream of cauliflower soup with items I had on hand. I was so touched that he came to care for me, and this soup reminds me of that special time.

—MILDRED LYNN CARUSO BRIGHTON, TN

START TO FINISH: 30 MIN.
MAKES: 6 SERVINGS

- 1 large head cauliflower, broken into florets
- 2 cans (14½ ounces each) chicken broth
- ½ cup heavy whipping cream
- ½ teaspoon ground nutmeg
- ½ teaspoon salt
- ⅛ teaspoon pepper
- 1 can (14 ounces) water-packed artichoke hearts, rinsed, drained and coarsely chopped
- ⅓ cup shredded Asiago cheese or Parmesan cheese
- 6 pieces bacon strips, cooked and crumbled

1. In a large saucepan, combine cauliflower and broth; bring to a boil. Reduce heat; cover and simmer for 10-15 minutes or until cauliflower is tender.
2. Cool slightly. In a blender, process soup in batches until smooth. Return all to the pan. Stir in the cream, nutmeg, salt and pepper; heat through. Serve with artichoke hearts, cheese and bacon.

Shortcut Split Pea Soup

Pair this soup with a simple tossed salad for a well-rounded, nourishing meal that's a breeze to prepare.

—DONNA NOEL GRAY, ME

START TO FINISH: 30 MIN.
MAKES: 5 SERVINGS

- 3 cups water
- 2 teaspoons reduced-sodium chicken bouillon granules
- ½ teaspoon dried thyme
- 4 celery ribs and leaves
- 2 medium carrots, thinly sliced
- 2 cans (11½ ounces each) condensed split pea soup, undiluted
- 1 cup cubed fully cooked ham
  Shaved Parmesan cheese, optional

1. In a large saucepan, bring the water, bouillon granules and thyme to a boil. Thinly slice celery ribs and finely chop the leaves; set leaves aside.
2. Add celery ribs and carrots to water mixture; simmer, uncovered, for 5-8 minutes or until tender. Stir in the soup, ham and celery leaves; heat through. Top each serving with cheese if desired.

Hot Italian Sausage Soup

I'm part owner of a small tavern, and our patrons love this soup loaded with fiery sausage and an array of veggies. A hint of brown sugar balances the heat with a little sweetness, making it a real crowd-pleaser.

—DAN BUTE OTTAWA, IL

START TO FINISH: 25 MIN.
MAKES: 4 SERVINGS

- 1 pound bulk hot Italian sausage
- 1 can (14½ ounces) Italian stewed tomatoes
- 1 can (8 ounces) tomato sauce
- 1 cup frozen Italian vegetables
- ¾ cup julienned green, sweet red and/or yellow pepper
- ¼ cup chopped onion
- ¼ cup white wine or chicken broth
- 1 teaspoon brown sugar
- 1 teaspoon minced fresh parsley
- ½ teaspoon Italian seasoning
- ⅛ teaspoon salt
- ⅛ teaspoon pepper

1. In a large skillet, cook sausage over medium heat until no longer pink.
2. Meanwhile, in a large saucepan, combine the remaining ingredients. Bring to a boil. Reduce heat; cover and simmer for 10 minutes or until vegetables are tender.
3. Drain sausage; add to soup and heat through.
4. Serve immediately or cool and transfer to freezer containers. May be frozen for up to 3 months.

HOT ITALIAN SAUSAGE SOUP

TUSCAN SAUSAGE AND POTATO SOUP

Tuscan Sausage and Potato Soup

This recipe feels extra special, but it's actually simple to make.

—**LISA SINICKI** ERIE, PA

PREP: 20 MIN. • **COOK:** 45 MIN.
MAKES: 10 SERVINGS (3¾ QUARTS)

- 1½ **pounds bulk Italian sausage**
- 3 **pounds potatoes, peeled and sliced**
- 3 **cans (14½ ounces each) chicken broth**
- 2 **cups water**
- 1 **cup chopped sweet onion**
- 2 **garlic cloves, minced**
- ¼ **teaspoon salt**
- ⅛ **teaspoon pepper**
- 3 **cups chopped Swiss chard**
- 2 **cups heavy whipping cream**
- 8 **bacon strips, cooked and crumbled**

1. In a large skillet, cook sausage over medium heat until no longer pink. Drain; set aside.
2. In a Dutch oven, combine the potatoes, broth, water, onion, garlic, salt and pepper. Bring to a boil. Reduce heat; cover and simmer for 18-22 minutes or until the potatoes are tender.
3. Stir in the Swiss chard, cream, bacon and sausage. Bring to a boil. Reduce heat; simmer, uncovered, for 5 to 10 minutes or until chard is tender.

Special French Onion Soup

I top this rich soup with Brie, prosciutto and garlic on French bread to make it extra appealing.

—**LAURA MCALLISTER** MORGANTON, NC

PREP: 1½ HOURS • **BAKE:** 10 MIN.
MAKES: 9 SERVINGS

- ¼ **cup butter, cubed**
- ¼ **cup plus 1 tablespoon olive oil, divided**
- 6 **large sweet onions, thinly sliced (about 12 cups)**
- 1 **whole garlic bulb**
- ¼ **cup dry red wine or beef broth**
- 6 **cups beef broth**
- 1½ **teaspoons Worcestershire sauce**
- 1 **bay leaf**
  Dash cayenne pepper
  Pepper to taste
- 9 **slices French bread (1 inch thick)**
- 1 **round (8 ounces) Brie cheese, rind removed, softened**
- 8 **thin slices prosciutto or deli ham, chopped**
- 2 **cups grated Parmesan cheese**

1. In a Dutch oven over medium heat, melt butter with ¼ cup oil; add onions. Cook, stirring occasionally, for 15 minutes. Reduce heat to low. Cook 45 minutes longer or until onions are golden, stirring occasionally.
2. Meanwhile, remove papery outer skin from garlic (do not peel or separate cloves). Cut top off garlic bulb; brush with remaining oil. Wrap in heavy-duty foil.
3. Bake at 425° for 30-35 minutes or until softened. Cool for 10-15 minutes. Squeeze softened garlic into a small bowl; mash and set aside.
4. Add wine to the onion mixture; cook for 2 minutes. Stir in the broth, Worcestershire sauce, bay leaf, cayenne and pepper. Bring to a boil. Reduce heat; simmer, uncovered, for 15-20 minutes.
5. Place bread on a baking sheet. Bake at 425° for 3-5 minutes or until golden brown, turning once. Spread each slice with Brie and mashed garlic; sprinkle with prosciutto.
6. Discard bay leaf from soup; ladle 1 cup each into nine ovenproof bowls. Top with one slice of toast; sprinkle with Parmesan cheese. Place bowls on a baking sheet. Bake for 10 minutes or until cheese is melted.

ITALIAN SAUSAGE & BEAN SOUP

1 cup half-and-half cream
Salt and pepper to taste
Grated Parmesan cheese, optional
Chopped fresh parsley, optional

1. Place asparagus in a large saucepan with enough water to cover; cook until crisp-tender. Drain and set aside.
2. In a large heavy saucepan, saute carrot in butter for 3-5 minutes; add onions and saute 2 minutes longer or until tender. Stir in flour; gradually add milk. Bring to a boil; boil and stir for 2 minutes. Add broth, ham, mushrooms and reserved asparagus. Reduce heat; add cream. Heat through but do not boil. Add salt and pepper. Garnish with Parmesan cheese and parsley if desired.

German Sauerkraut Soup

My mother used to make this soup quite often while I was growing up. I added my own touch, spicing it up a bit with the bacon and smoked sausage.
—**THELMA LESCHENKO** EDMONTON, AB

PREP: 2 HOURS • **COOK:** 40 MIN.
MAKES: 12 SERVINGS (3 QUARTS)

- 2 **pounds pork spareribs**
- 3 **quarts water**
- 2 **cups diced peeled potatoes**
- 2 **carrots, chopped**
- 1 **teaspoon salt**
- ½ **teaspoon pepper**
- 4 **cups sauerkraut, rinsed and drained**
- 1 **pound smoked sausage, cut into 1-inch slices**
- 5 **bacon strips, diced**
- 1 **large onion, chopped**

1. In a Dutch oven, cook ribs in water until tender, about 1½ hours. Skim off foam. Remove ribs from broth; strain broth and skim fat.
2. Return broth to the heat. Add the potatoes, carrots, salt and pepper; simmer until vegetables are tender. Remove meat from bones and add to broth with the sauerkraut and sausage.
3. Meanwhile, cook bacon until crisp; remove to paper towels to drain. Discard all but 1 tablespoon of the drippings. Cook onion in drippings until tender. Add to soup; cook 20-30 minutes longer. Ladle into bowls. Garnish with bacon.

⑤ INGREDIENTS Italian Sausage & Bean Soup

The unusual blend of sausage and beans with coleslaw makes this soup the definition of complete comfort food. The recipe doubles easily to serve a large group. Pair the soup with a warm loaf of bread and a tossed salad.
—**STACEY BENNETT** LOCUST GROVE, VA

START TO FINISH: 30 MIN.
MAKES: 6 SERVINGS (2 QUARTS)

- 1 **pound bulk hot Italian sausage**
- 2 **cans (15½ ounces each) great northern beans, rinsed and drained**
- 1 **package (16 ounces) coleslaw mix**
- 1 **jar (24 ounces) garlic and herb spaghetti sauce**
- 3 **cups water**

In a Dutch oven, cook sausage over medium heat until no longer pink; drain. Stir in the remaining ingredients. Bring to a boil. Reduce heat; simmer, uncovered, for 16-20 minutes or until flavors are blended.

Creamy Ham and Asparagus Soup

When I have to bake a large ham, I save the leftovers for this recipe. Fresh asparagus really perks up the broth.
—**MAURINE KENT** KILGORE, TX

START TO FINISH: 30 MIN.
MAKES: 4 SERVINGS

- 1½ **cups cut fresh asparagus (1-inch pieces)**
- 1 **medium carrot, julienned**
- 2 **tablespoons butter**
- 3 **small onions, quartered**
- 2 **tablespoons all-purpose flour**
- 1 **cup milk**
- 1 **cup chicken broth**
- 1 **cup cubed fully cooked ham**
- 1 **jar (2½ ounces) sliced mushrooms, drained**

CREAMY VEGETABLE CHOWDER

Creamy Vegetable Chowder

This rich, comforting soup has it all. If you'd like, you can lower the fat content by using turkey bacon, vegetable broth and skim milk. It's delicious either way.

—SUZANNA VANDEBRAKE PEYTON, CO

PREP: 30 MIN. • **COOK:** 1 HOUR
MAKES: 12 SERVINGS (3 QUARTS)

- ¾ **pound sliced bacon, chopped**
- 2 **large onions**
- 2 **medium carrots**
- 2 **celery ribs**
- 2 **medium parsnips**
- 2 **small turnips**
- ¾ **cup all-purpose flour**
- ½ **teaspoon salt**
- ½ **teaspoon cayenne pepper**
- 2 **cartons (32 ounces each) chicken broth**
- 1 **medium sweet potato, peeled and chopped**
- 3 **small red potatoes, chopped**
- 2 **bay leaves**
- 1 **tablespoon Worcestershire sauce**
- ¼ **teaspoon hot pepper sauce**
- 1 **cup half-and-half cream**
- ½ **cup minced fresh parsley**

1. In a Dutch oven, cook bacon over medium heat until crisp. Remove to paper towels; drain, reserving 3 tablespoons drippings. Chop the onions, carrots, celery, parsnips and turnips; add to the pan. Cook and stir for 6-8 minutes or until fragrant.
2. Sprinkle vegetables with flour, salt and cayenne; stir until blended. Gradually add broth. Bring to a boil; cook and stir for 2 minutes or until thickened. Stir in the sweet potato, potatoes, bay leaves, Worcestershire sauce and pepper sauce.
3. Reduce heat; cover and simmer for 15-20 minutes or until potatoes are tender. Stir in cream and parsley; heat through. Discard bay leaves.

Confetti Soup

My family members weren't big veggie eaters before I created this recipe, but now they eat this up!
—NANCY OLSON BELGRADE, MN

START TO FINISH: 30 MIN.
MAKES: 8 SERVINGS (2 QUARTS)

- 1 **cup diced carrots**
- 1 **cup diced rutabaga**
- ½ **cup chopped celery**
- ½ **cup fresh broccoli florets**
- ½ **cup fresh cauliflowerets**
- ½ **cup chopped onion**
- 3 **tablespoons water**
- 3 **tablespoons butter, optional**
- 1 **cup process cheese (Velveeta), cubed**
- 1 **cup frozen whole kernel corn**
- ½ **cup frozen peas**
- ½ **cup cubed fully cooked ham**
- 5 **cups milk**
- 1½ **teaspoons salt**
- ½ **teaspoon pepper**
- ¼ **teaspoon sugar**

1. In a microwave-safe 3-qt. baking dish, combine carrots, rutabaga, celery, broccoli, cauliflower, onion, water and butter if desired. Cover and microwave on high for 9 minutes or until vegetables are just tender, stirring three times during cooking.
2. Stir in cheese, corn, peas and ham; cover and let stand for 1 minute. Add milk, salt, pepper and sugar; cover and microwave on medium-high, stirring three times, for 5-7 minutes or until cheese is melted and soup is heated through (do not boil).
NOTE *This recipe was tested in a 1,100-watt microwave.*

Buy rutabagas that are **heavy, smooth-skinned, and not spongy.** Don't wash the rutabagas until just **before using them** in a recipe.

PEPPERONI PIZZA CHILI

Pepperoni Pizza Chili

Pizza and chili go together—what could be better? Fill folks up when you set out bowls of this change-of-pace delight!
—**JENNIFER GELORMINO** PITTSBURGH, PA

PREP: 20 MIN. • **COOK:** 30 MIN.
MAKES: 12 SERVINGS (3 QUARTS)

- 2 **pounds ground beef**
- 1 **pound bulk hot Italian sausage**
- 1 **large onion, chopped**
- 1 **large green pepper, chopped**
- 4 **garlic cloves, minced**
- 1 **jar (16 ounces) salsa**
- 1 **can (16 ounces) hot chili beans, undrained**
- 1 **can (16 ounces) kidney beans, rinsed and drained**
- 1 **can (12 ounces) pizza sauce**
- 1 **package (8 ounces) sliced pepperoni, halved**
- 1 **cup water**
- 2 **teaspoons chili powder**
- ½ **teaspoon salt**
- ½ **teaspoon pepper**
- 3 **cups (12 ounces) shredded part-skim mozzarella cheese**

1. In a Dutch oven, cook the beef, sausage, onion, green pepper and garlic over medium heat until meat is no longer pink; drain.
2. Stir in the salsa, beans, pizza sauce, pepperoni, water, chili powder, salt and pepper. Bring to a boil. Reduce heat; cover and simmer for 20 minutes or until heated through. Sprinkle servings with cheese.

Jamaican Ham and Bean Soup

"Island vacation in a bowl" might be the best way to describe this hearty soup. A splash of lime juice and a hint of jerk seasoning add tropical taste.
—**MARY LOU TIMPSON** COLORADO CITY, AZ

START TO FINISH: 30 MIN.
MAKES: 7 SERVINGS

- 1 **small onion, chopped**
- 1 **tablespoon canola oil**
- 3 **cups cubed fully cooked ham**
- 2 **cans (16 ounces each) vegetarian refried beans**
- 1 **can (14½ ounces) chicken broth**
- 1 **can (11 ounces) Mexicorn, drained**
- 1 **can (7 ounces) white or shoepeg corn, drained**
- 1 **can (4 ounces) chopped green chilies**
- ½ **cup salsa**
- 1 **teaspoon Caribbean jerk seasoning**
- 1 **can (2¼ ounces) sliced ripe olives, drained**
- ⅓ **cup lime juice**
  Sour cream and lime slices

1. In a Dutch oven, saute onion in oil for 3-4 minutes or until tender. Stir in the ham, refried beans, broth, corn, chilies, salsa and jerk seasoning; bring to a boil. Reduce heat; simmer, uncovered, for 5 minutes, stirring occasionally.
2. Stir in the olives and lime juice; heat through. Garnish servings with sour cream and lime slices.

Favorite Italian Sausage Stew

Answer those "what's for dinner?" questions with ease! This heartwarming chili is table-ready in just 45 minutes.

—TASTE OF HOME TEST KITCHEN

PREP: 15 MIN. • **COOK:** 30 MIN.
MAKES: 4 SERVINGS

- ½ **pound bulk Italian sausage**
- 2 **garlic cloves, minced**
- 1 **tablespoon cornstarch**
- 1 **can (14½ ounces) reduced-sodium beef broth**
- 1 **can (14½ ounces) Italian diced tomatoes**
- 4 **small red potatoes, quartered**
- ¼ **cup sliced fresh carrots**
- 1 **tablespoon minced fresh basil**
- ½ **cup sliced zucchini**
- ¼ **cup shredded Parmesan cheese, optional**

1. In a large saucepan, cook sausage over medium heat until meat is no longer pink. Add garlic; cook 1 minute longer. Drain. Combine the cornstarch and broth until smooth; stir into sausage mixture. Add the tomatoes, potatoes, carrots and basil. Bring to a boil. Reduce heat; add zucchini.

2. Cover and simmer for about 15 minutes or until vegetables are tender. Sprinkle with Parmesan if desired.

Kielbasa Spinach Soup

When it comes to meal-in-a-bowl soups, this is one of the best. Collard greens or chopped kale can be used instead of spinach. The hot pepper sauce adds real kick, but it's fine to leave it out and let each person flavor his or her own serving.

—ANTOINETTE PISICCHIO EASTON, PA

START TO FINISH: 20 MIN.
MAKES: 4 SERVINGS

- 1 **carton (32 ounces) chicken broth**
- 1 **package (10 ounces) frozen chopped spinach**
- ½ **pound smoked kielbasa or Polish sausage, halved and sliced**
- 1 **can (15 ounces) white kidney or cannellini beans, rinsed and drained**
- ⅔ **cup uncooked elbow macaroni**
- 8 **to 10 drops hot pepper sauce**

Combine the broth, spinach and kielbasa in a large saucepan. Bring to a boil. Add beans and macaroni. Reduce heat; simmer, uncovered, for 7-9 minutes or until macaroni is tender. Stir in pepper sauce.

FAVORITE ITALIAN SAUSAGE STEW

Meatless

57   60   59

Whether you're serving a vegetarian crowd or just want to switch up the menu, **dare to go meatless.** Dip your spoon into a thick tomato soup, a tasty gazpacho or even a refreshingly fruity specialty. With flavors this enticing and recipes this easy, you'll have to **sample them all.**

ROASTED TOMATO SOUP

1 large onion, finely chopped
2 tablespoons olive oil
1 tablespoon butter
2 garlic cloves, minced
2 teaspoons ground cumin
1 cinnamon stick (3 inches)
½ teaspoon chili powder
4 cups vegetable broth
2 cups cubed peeled butternut squash
1 can (15 ounces) chickpeas or garbanzo beans, rinsed and drained
1 can (14½ ounces) diced tomatoes, undrained
1 medium red potato, cut into 1-inch cubes
1 medium sweet potato, peeled and cut into 1-inch cubes
1 medium lemon, thinly sliced
¼ teaspoon salt
2 small zucchini, cubed
3 tablespoons minced fresh cilantro

1. In a Dutch oven, saute onion in oil and butter until tender. Add the garlic, cumin, cinnamon stick and chili powder; saute 1 minute longer.
2. Stir in the broth, squash, chickpeas, tomatoes, potatoes, lemon and salt. Bring to a boil. Reduce heat; cover and simmer for 15-20 minutes or until potatoes and squash are almost tender.
3. Add zucchini; return to a boil. Reduce heat; cover and simmer for 5-8 minutes or until vegetables are tender. Discard cinnamon stick and lemon slices. Stir in cilantro.

Roasted Tomato Soup

After we gather up all of the tomatoes from my mom's garden, we create this flavor-packed soup. Although it sounds like a lot, the garlic becomes mellow and almost sweet when roasted.

—KAITLYN LERDAHL MADISON, WI

PREP: 25 MIN. • **COOK:** 40 MIN.
MAKES: 6 SERVINGS

15 large tomatoes (5 pounds), seeded and quartered
¼ cup plus 2 tablespoons canola oil, divided
8 garlic cloves, minced
1 large onion, chopped
2 cups water
1 teaspoon salt
½ teaspoon crushed red pepper flakes, optional
½ cup heavy whipping cream
Fresh basil leaves, optional

1. Place tomatoes in a greased 15-in. x 10-in. x 1-in. baking pan. Combine ¼ cup oil and garlic; drizzle over tomatoes. Toss to coat. Bake at 400° for 15-20 minutes or until softened, stirring occasionally. Remove and discard skins.
2. Meanwhile, in a Dutch oven, saute onion in remaining oil until tender. Add the tomatoes, water, salt and, if desired, pepper flakes. Bring to a boil. Reduce heat; cover and simmer for 30 minutes. Cool slightly.
3. In a blender, process soup in batches until smooth. Stir in cream and heat through. Top with basil if desired and serve immediately; or cool soup and transfer to freezer containers. Cover and freeze for up to 3 months.

Moroccan Chickpea Stew

When I served this spicy stew to friends, both vegetarians and nonvegetarians, they were thrilled with the abundance of squash, potatoes, tomatoes and zucchini.

—CINDY BEBERMAN ORLAND PARK, IL

PREP: 20 MIN. • **COOK:** 30 MIN.
MAKES: 9 SERVINGS (ABOUT 2 QUARTS)

SOUTHWESTERN BEAN CHOWDER

in the mashed beans, broth, corn, carrot, chilies, cumin, chili powder and remaining beans. Bring to a boil. Reduce heat; simmer, uncovered, for 20 minutes.

3. Combine cornstarch and milk until smooth. Stir into bean mixture. Bring to a boil; cook and stir for 2 minutes or until thickened. Stir in cheese until melted. Serve with cilantro and additional cheese if desired.

So Easy Gazpacho

My daughter got this recipe from a friend and I'm glad she shared it with me. Now I serve it often as an appetizer, and it's certainly the talk of the party.

—LORNA SIRTOLI CORTLAND, NY

PREP: 10 MIN. + CHILLING
MAKES: 5 SERVINGS

- 2 **cups tomato juice**
- 4 **medium tomatoes, peeled and finely chopped**
- ½ **cup chopped seeded peeled cucumber**
- ⅓ **cup finely chopped onion**
- ¼ **cup olive oil**
- ¼ **cup cider vinegar**
- 1 **teaspoon sugar**
- 1 **garlic clove, minced**
- ¼ **teaspoon salt**
- ¼ **teaspoon pepper**

In a large bowl, combine all ingredients. Cover and refrigerate at least 4 hours or until chilled.

Southwestern Bean Chowder

My young children love this soup as much as my husband does. I like using white kidney beans because they have a terrific texture.

—JULI MEYERS HINESVILLE, GA

PREP: 20 MIN. • **COOK:** 35 MIN.
MAKES: 8 SERVINGS (2 QUARTS)

- 2 **cans (15 ounces each) white kidney or cannellini beans, rinsed and drained, divided**
- 1 **medium onion, chopped**
- ¼ **cup chopped celery**
- ¼ **cup chopped green pepper**
- 1 **tablespoon olive oil**
- 2 **garlic cloves, minced**
- 3 **cups vegetable broth**
- 1½ **cups frozen corn, thawed**
- 1 **medium carrot, shredded**
- 1 **can (4 ounces) chopped green chilies**
- 1 **tablespoon ground cumin**
- ½ **teaspoon chili powder**
- 4½ **teaspoons cornstarch**
- 2 **cups 2% milk**
- 1 **cup (4 ounces) shredded cheddar cheese**
  Minced fresh cilantro and additional shredded cheddar cheese, optional

1. In a small bowl, mash one can beans with a fork; set aside.

2. In a Dutch oven, saute the onion, celery and pepper in oil until tender. Add garlic; cook 1 minute longer. Stir

Pumpkin Corn Soup

My family can't get enough of this meal, especially on cold winter nights. It's definitely not your typical soup. Fresh cilantro makes for a nice garnish.

—**MELISSA EVERY** AUSTIN, TX

PREP: 20 MIN. • **COOK:** 25 MIN.
MAKES: 7 SERVINGS

- 1 **large onion, chopped**
- 1 **medium sweet red pepper, chopped**
- 2 **tablespoons butter**
- 2 **cups fresh or frozen corn, thawed**
- 1 **jalapeno pepper, seeded and chopped**
- 2 **garlic cloves, minced**
- 2 **teaspoons chili powder**
- 2 **cans (14½ ounces each) vegetable broth**
- 1 **can (15 ounces) solid-pack pumpkin**
- ½ **teaspoon salt**
  Dash cayenne pepper
- 2 **tablespoons lime juice**

1. In a large saucepan, saute the onion and red pepper in butter until almost tender. Add the corn, jalapeno, garlic and chili powder; saute 2 minutes longer.
2. Stir in the broth, pumpkin, salt and cayenne until blended. Bring to a boil. Reduce heat; cover and simmer for 10 minutes. Stir in lime juice.
NOTE *Wear disposable gloves when cutting hot peppers; the oils can burn skin. Avoid touching your face.*

Veggie Tortellini Soup

Italian cuisine has more to offer than just spaghetti and pizza—check out this mouthwatering, healthy soup! I've served it to company for years, and they usually ask for a copy of the recipe when they're done.

—**PRISCILLA GILBERT**
INDIAN HARBOUR BEACH, FL

PREP: 15 MIN. • **COOK:** 20 MIN.
MAKES: 7 SERVINGS

- 3 **medium carrots, chopped**
- 1 **large onion, chopped**
- 1 **tablespoon olive oil**
- 4 **garlic cloves, minced**
- 2 **cans (14½ ounces each) vegetable broth**
- 2 **medium zucchini, chopped**
- 4 **plum tomatoes, chopped**
- 2 **cups refrigerated cheese tortellini**
- ⅓ **cup chopped fresh spinach**
- 1 **teaspoon minced fresh rosemary or ¼ teaspoon dried rosemary, crushed**
- ¼ **teaspoon pepper**
- 1 **tablespoon red wine vinegar**

1. In a Dutch oven, saute carrots and onion in oil until onion is tender. Add garlic; cook 1 minute longer.
2. Stir in the broth, zucchini, tomatoes, tortellini, spinach, rosemary and pepper. Bring to a boil. Reduce heat; cover and simmer for 8-10 minutes or until tortellini are tender. Just before serving, stir in vinegar.

VEGGIE TORTELLINI SOUP

Meatless Lentil Soup

My husband has enjoyed this soup for years now. He takes a thermos full of it to work for lunch during the winter.

—**JANET CHASE** BERRIEN SPRINGS, MI

PREP: 15 MIN. • **COOK:** 35 MIN.
MAKES: 8 SERVINGS (3 QUARTS)

- 2 **large carrots, halved and sliced**
- 2 **celery ribs, sliced**
- 1 **medium onion, chopped**
- 10 **cups water**
- 1 **package (16 ounces) dried lentils, rinsed**
- 4 **small red potatoes, diced**
- 2 **bay leaves**
- 2 **teaspoons salt**
- 1 **teaspoon pepper**

1. In a large nonstick saucepan coated with cooking spray, cook the carrots, celery and onion over medium heat for 5 minutes.
2. Stir in the water, lentils, potatoes, bay leaves, salt and pepper. Bring to a boil. Reduce heat; cover and simmer for 30-35 minutes or until lentils are tender. Discard bay leaves.

ASPARAGUS SOUP WITH LEMON CREME FRAICHE

Kale & Bean Soup

Full of veggies, this soup soothes both the body and the spirit. The kale is packed with nutrients, and the beans add a natural creaminess.

—**BETH SOLLARS** DELRAY BEACH, FL

PREP: 20 MIN. • **COOK:** 70 MIN.
MAKES: 8 SERVINGS (2½ QUARTS)

- 2 **medium onions, chopped**
- 2 **cups cubed peeled potatoes**
- 1 **tablespoon olive oil**
- 4 **garlic cloves, minced**
- 1 **bunch kale, trimmed and coarsely chopped**
- 3½ **cups vegetable broth**
- 1 **can (28 ounces) diced tomatoes, undrained**
- 1½ **cups water**
- 1 **teaspoon Italian seasoning**
- 1 **teaspoon paprika**
- ½ **teaspoon pepper**
- 1 **bay leaf**
- 1 **can (15 ounces) white kidney or cannellini beans, rinsed and drained**

1. In a Dutch oven, saute onions and potatoes in oil until tender. Add garlic; cook 1 minute longer. Stir in the kale, broth, tomatoes, water, Italian seasoning, paprika, pepper and bay leaf. Bring to a boil. Reduce heat; cover and simmer for 50-60 minutes or until kale is tender.
2. Cool slightly. Discard bay leaf. In a blender, process 3 cups soup until smooth. Return to pan; add beans and heat through.

Asparagus Soup with Lemon Creme Fraiche

Pureed asparagus makes for an incredible soup. Serve it warm or chilled, depending on the weather or your personal preference.

—**FERN VITENSE** TIPTON, IA

PREP: 25 MIN. • **COOK:** 25 MIN.
MAKES: 6 SERVINGS

- 1 **tablespoon butter**
- 1 **tablespoon olive oil**
- 1 **small onion, chopped**
- 4 **cups cut fresh asparagus (1-inch pieces)**
- 3 **medium red potatoes, peeled and cubed**
- 2 **cans (14½ ounces each) vegetable broth**
- 2 **teaspoons grated lemon peel**
- ½ **teaspoon salt**
- ½ **teaspoon pepper**
- ½ **teaspoon ground coriander**
- ¼ **teaspoon ground ginger**

GARNISH
- ¼ **cup minced chives**
- ¼ **cup creme fraiche or sour cream**
- 1 **tablespoon lemon juice**
- ½ **teaspoon grated lemon peel**

1. In a large saucepan, heat butter and oil over medium-high heat. Add onion; cook and stir until tender. Add asparagus and potatoes; cook 3 minutes longer. Stir in broth, lemon peel and seasonings. Bring to a boil. Reduce heat; simmer, covered, 15-20 minutes or until potatoes are tender.
2. Cool slightly. Process soup in batches in a blender until smooth. Return all to pan and heat through. Combine garnish ingredients; serve with soup.

Ginger Butternut Squash Bisque

This soup is filling enough for even my hungry husband. We've been hooked ever since some friends made it for us.

—CARA MCDONALD WINTER PARK, CO

PREP: 25 MIN. • **BAKE:** 40 MIN. + COOLING
MAKES: 6 SERVINGS

- 1 **medium butternut squash (about 3 pounds)**
- 1 **tablespoon olive oil**
- 2 **medium carrots, finely chopped**
- 1 **medium onion, chopped**
- 2 **garlic cloves, minced**
- 2 **teaspoons minced fresh gingerroot**
- 2 **teaspoons curry powder**
- 1 **can (14½ ounces) vegetable broth**
- 1 **can (13.66 ounces) coconut milk**
- 1 **teaspoon salt**
- ½ **teaspoon pepper**
- 2 **cups hot cooked brown rice**
- ¼ **cup flaked coconut, toasted**
- ¼ **cup salted peanuts, coarsely chopped**
- ¼ **cup minced fresh cilantro**

1. Preheat oven to 400°. Cut squash lengthwise in half; remove and discard seeds. Place squash in a greased shallow roasting pan, cut side down. Roast 40-45 minutes or until squash is tender. Cool slightly.

2. In a large saucepan, heat oil over medium heat. Add carrots and onion; cook and stir until tender. Add garlic, ginger and curry powder; cook and stir 1 minute longer. Add broth; bring to a boil. Reduce heat; simmer, uncovered, 10-12 minutes or until carrots are tender.

3. Scoop pulp from squash; discard skins. Add squash, coconut milk, salt and pepper to carrot mixture; bring just to a boil, stirring occasionally. Remove from heat; cool slightly. Process in batches in a blender until smooth.

4. Return to pan; heat through. Top servings with rice, coconut, peanuts and cilantro.

NOTE *To toast coconut, spread in a dry skillet; cook and stir over low heat until lightly browned.*

Potato-Lentil Stew

Jam-packed with veggies, this main-dish soup equals a meal the whole family will love. Serve with a loaf of your favorite bread, and dinner's done!

—KRISTA GOODWIN YPSILANTI, MI

PREP: 20 MIN. • **COOK:** 40 MIN.
MAKES: 6 SERVINGS (2½ QUARTS)

- 1 **large onion, chopped**
- 2 **medium carrots, chopped**
- 2 **teaspoons olive oil**
- 4 **teaspoons chili powder**
- 3 **garlic cloves, minced**
- 3 **teaspoons ground cumin**
- 1 **teaspoon dried oregano**
- 1 **carton (32 ounces) vegetable broth**
- ¾ **cup dried lentils, rinsed**
- 2 **cans (10 ounces each) diced tomatoes and green chilies**
- 3½ **cups frozen cubed hash brown potatoes**
- 1 **can (16 ounces) kidney beans, rinsed and drained**
- ½ **teaspoon salt**
- ¼ **teaspoon pepper**

1. In a Dutch oven, saute onion and carrots in oil for 3 minutes. Add the chili powder, garlic, cumin and oregano; cook 1 minute longer.

2. Stir in broth and lentils. Bring to a boil. Reduce heat; cover and simmer for 20-22 minutes or until lentils are tender. Stir in the tomatoes, potatoes, beans, salt and pepper. Return to a boil. Reduce heat; cover and simmer 10-15 minutes longer or until potatoes are tender.

GINGER BUTTERNUT SQUASH BISQUE

LIMA BEAN OKRA SOUP

Lima Bean Okra Soup

This soup's special appeal comes from the wonderful combination of vegetables with a hint of sweet spices. Every brightly colored serving is loaded with goodness.

—CLARA COULSON MINNEY
WASHINGTON COURT HOUSE, OH

PREP: 20 MIN. • **COOK:** 15 MIN.
MAKES: 7 SERVINGS

- 1 **medium green pepper, chopped**
- 1 **medium onion, chopped**
- ¼ **teaspoon whole cloves**
- 1 **tablespoon butter**
- 3 **cups vegetable broth**
- 3 **cups chopped tomatoes**
- 2½ **cups sliced fresh or frozen okra, thawed**
- 1 **cup frozen lima beans, thawed**
- ½ **cup fresh or frozen corn, thawed**
- ½ to 1 **teaspoon salt**
- ¼ to ½ **teaspoon ground allspice**
- ¼ **teaspoon pepper**
- ⅛ **teaspoon cayenne pepper**

1. In a large saucepan, saute the green pepper, onion and cloves in butter until vegetables are tender. Discard cloves.
2. Stir in the remaining ingredients. Bring to a boil. Reduce heat; cover and simmer for 15-20 minutes or until beans are tender.

Spicy Couscous & Tomato Soup

Bring some Middle Eastern flavors to your table with this recipe. It's good for you, too, so there's no guilt involved.

—RITA COMBS VALDOSTA, GA

PREP: 15 MIN. • **COOK:** 40 MIN.
MAKES: 7 SERVINGS

- 2 **medium sweet yellow peppers, chopped**
- 1 **medium red onion, chopped**
- 2½ **teaspoons olive oil**
- 3 **garlic cloves, minced**
- 6 **cups vegetable broth**
- 6 **plum tomatoes, chopped**
- 1½ **teaspoons ground cumin**
- 1½ **teaspoons ground coriander**
- ½ **teaspoon ground cinnamon**
- ½ **teaspoon cayenne pepper**
- ¼ **teaspoon pepper**
- ½ **cup uncooked couscous**

1. In a Dutch oven, saute peppers and onion in oil until tender. Add garlic; cook 1 minute longer. Stir in the broth, tomatoes, cumin, coriander, cinnamon, cayenne and pepper. Bring to a boil. Reduce heat; cover and simmer for 20-25 minutes or until flavors are blended.
2. Stir in couscous; cover and cook 4-6 minutes longer or until couscous is tender.

Vegetarian Polka Dot Stew

If you like traditional minestrone, you'll enjoy this stew. The fun polka-dot shapes come from the couscous, black beans and sliced baby carrots.

—TEAGAN O'TOOLE BOSTON, MA

START TO FINISH: 30 MIN.
MAKES: 5 SERVINGS

- 2 **cups water**
- 1 **cup uncooked pearl (Israeli) couscous**
- 2 **medium carrots, sliced**
- 1 **plum tomato, chopped**
- ¼ **cup chopped onion**
- 1 **garlic clove, minced**
- 2 **cans (19 ounces each) ready-to-serve tomato soup**
- 1 **can (15 ounces) black beans, rinsed and drained**
- 1 **package (10 ounces) frozen chopped spinach, thawed and squeezed dry**
- 1 **tablespoon minced fresh basil or 1 teaspoon dried basil**
- ½ **teaspoon salt**
- ½ **teaspoon dried oregano**
- ½ **teaspoon dried marjoram**
- ¼ **teaspoon pepper**
  Shredded Parmesan cheese

In a large saucepan, bring water to a boil. Stir in the couscous, carrots, tomato, onion and garlic. Bring to a boil. Reduce heat; simmer, uncovered, for 10-15 minutes or until tender and water is absorbed. Stir in the remaining ingredients; heat through. Sprinkle with cheese.
NOTE *You may substitute 1 cup quick-cooking barley for the couscous if desired.*

VEGETARIAN POLKA DOT STEW

Hearty Quinoa & Corn Chowder

My grandmother lived in the Appalachian Mountains and always served straight-from-the-garden corn and beans. I created this soup to reflect some of her best meals, then added quinoa and herbs.

—**KARI NAPIER** LOUISVILLE, KY

PREP: 25 MIN. + STANDING • **COOK:** 15 MIN.
MAKES: 14 SERVINGS (¾ CUP EACH)

- 3 **medium sweet red peppers**
- 1 **cup quinoa, rinsed**
- 1 **tablespoon butter**
- 1 **tablespoon olive oil**
- 1 **medium onion, chopped**
- 2 **garlic cloves, minced**
- ⅓ **cup all-purpose flour**
- 4 **cups vegetable stock**
- 2 **cups heavy whipping cream**
- 6 **medium ears sweet corn, kernels removed (about 4 cups), or 2 packages (10 ounces) frozen corn, thawed**
- 1 **can (15 ounces) pinto beans, rinsed and drained**
- 2 **tablespoons minced fresh parsley**
- ½ **teaspoon minced fresh thyme**
- 1½ **teaspoons salt**
- ½ **teaspoon pepper**

1. Broil peppers 4 in. from the heat until skins blister, about 5 minutes. With tongs, rotate peppers a quarter turn. Broil and rotate until all sides are blistered and blackened. Immediately place peppers in a large bowl; cover and let stand for 20 minutes.
2. Peel off and discard charred skin. Remove the stems and seeds. Finely chop peppers.
3. Meanwhile, in a Dutch oven, cook and stir quinoa over medium-high heat for 3-5 minutes or until lightly toasted; remove from the pan.
4. In the same pan, heat butter and oil over medium-high heat. Add onion; cook and stir until tender. Add garlic; cook 1 minute longer. Stir in flour until blended. Gradually whisk in stock and cream.
5. Add corn, beans, roasted peppers and quinoa; bring to a boil, stirring frequently. Reduce heat; simmer, uncovered, for 15-20 minutes or until quinoa is tender, stirring occasionally. Stir in the remaining ingredients.

Miso Soup with Tofu and Enoki

This traditional Japanese soup is soothing and mild, and made with easy-to-find ingredients. Sliced green onions give it a nice table presentation.

—**BRIDGET KLUSMAN** OTSEGO, MI

START TO FINISH: 30 MIN.
MAKES: 5 SERVINGS

- 2 **packages (3½ ounces each) fresh enoki mushrooms or ½ pound sliced fresh mushrooms**
- 1 **medium onion, chopped**
- 2 **garlic cloves, minced**
- 1 **teaspoon minced fresh gingerroot**
- 1 **tablespoon canola oil**
- 4 **cups water**
- ¼ **cup miso paste**
- 1 **package (16 ounces) firm tofu, drained and cut into ¾-inch cubes Thinly sliced green onions**

In a Dutch oven, saute mushrooms, onion, garlic and ginger in oil until tender. Add the water and miso paste. Bring to a boil. Reduce heat; simmer, uncovered, for 15 minutes. Add tofu; heat through. Ladle into bowls; garnish with green onions.
NOTE *Look for miso paste in natural food or Asian markets.*

Clean mushrooms for cooking by gently rubbing with a **mushroom brush** or wipe them with a damp paper towel. Then they're **ready to go.**

MISO SOUP WITH TOFU AND ENOKI

SPICY PEANUT SOUP

1 medium ripe avocado, peeled and finely chopped
9 tablespoons reduced-fat sour cream

1. In a Dutch oven, saute the mushrooms, onion and sun-dried tomatoes in oil until tender. Add garlic; cook 1 minute longer. Add meat crumbles; heat through.

2. Stir in the chili beans, tomatoes, water, broth, chili powder, brown sugar, celery salt and cumin. Bring to a boil. Reduce heat; simmer, uncovered, for 10 minutes. Ladle chili into bowls. Top each serving with avocado and sour cream.

NOTE *Vegetarian meat crumbles are a nutritious protein source made from soy. Look for them in the natural foods freezer section.*

Spicy Peanut Soup

After enjoying a spicy peanut soup at a little cafe, I knew I had to duplicate it at home. I think my version comes pretty close!

—LISA MEREDITH ST. PAUL, MN

PREP: 35 MIN. • **COOK:** 20 MIN.
MAKES: 7 SERVINGS

2 medium carrots, chopped
1 small onion, chopped
2 tablespoons olive oil
2 garlic cloves, minced
1 large sweet potato, peeled and cubed
½ cup chunky peanut butter
2 tablespoons red curry paste
2 cans (14½ ounces each) vegetable broth
1 can (14½ ounces) fire-roasted diced tomatoes, undrained
1 bay leaf
1 fresh thyme sprig
½ teaspoon pepper
½ cup unsalted peanuts

1. In a large saucepan, cook the carrots and onion in oil over medium heat for 2 minutes. Add garlic; cook 1 minute longer.
2. Stir in the sweet potato; cook 2 minutes longer. Stir in peanut butter and curry paste until blended. Add the broth, tomatoes, bay leaf, thyme and pepper.

3. Bring to a boil. Reduce heat; cover and simmer for 15-20 minutes or until sweet potatoes and carrots are tender. (Soup will appear curdled.) Discard bay leaf and thyme sprig. Stir soup until blended. Sprinkle with peanuts.

Hearty Vegetarian Chili

Packed with mushrooms, beans, sun-dried tomatoes and more, this chili recipe is so satisfying, you won't even miss the meat.

—PAM IVBULS OMAHA, NE

START TO FINISH: 30 MIN.
MAKES: 9 SERVINGS (2¼ QUARTS)

1¾ cups chopped baby portobello mushrooms
1 medium onion, finely chopped
½ cup chopped sun-dried tomatoes (not packed in oil)
2 tablespoons olive oil
2 garlic cloves, minced
1 package (12 ounces) frozen vegetarian meat crumbles
2 cans (16 ounces each) chili beans, undrained
2 cans (14½ ounces each) no-salt-added diced tomatoes
½ cup water
½ cup vegetable broth
4½ teaspoons chili powder
2 teaspoons brown sugar
½ teaspoon celery salt
½ teaspoon ground cumin

Watermelon Gazpacho

Nothing cools off the hot days of summer like a bowl of this refreshing watermelon soup. Its subtle sweetness, touch of mint and pretty pink color make it so appealing.

—JILL SPARROW INDIANAPOLIS, IN

PREP: 20 MIN. + CHILLING
MAKES: 9 SERVINGS (2¼ QUARTS)

½ cup sugar
½ cup water
12 cups seeded chopped watermelon
2 cups chopped honeydew
½ cup fresh mint leaves
¼ cup lime juice
1 teaspoon salt
TOPPING
½ cup sour cream
2 tablespoons sugar

1. In a small saucepan, combine sugar and water. Bring to a boil over medium heat. Reduce heat; simmer, uncovered, for 2-3 minutes or until sugar is dissolved, stirring occasionally. Remove from the heat; cool to room temperature.
2. Working in batches if necessary, place the sugar mixture, watermelon, honeydew, mint, lime juice and salt in a food processor. Cover and process until smooth. Refrigerate for at least 2 hours.
3. Combine sour cream and sugar. Garnish each serving with topping.

BULGUR CHILI

Bulgur Chili

This vegetarian chili is zesty, but it also offers a slight hint of sweetness. Because it doesn't have to simmer for hours like other chili recipes, it's ideal for when you have drop-in visitors.

—JERALDINE HALL RAVENDEN SPRINGS, AR

PREP: 10 MIN. + STANDING • **COOK:** 25 MIN.
MAKES: 9 SERVINGS

- ¾ cup bulgur
- 2 cups boiling water
- 1½ cups finely chopped green peppers
- 1 large onion, chopped
- 2 teaspoons canola oil
- 2 cups reduced-sodium tomato juice
- 1 can (16 ounces) kidney beans, rinsed and drained
- 1 can (15 ounces) Ranch Style beans (pinto beans in seasoned tomato sauce)
- 1 can (14½ ounces) diced tomatoes, undrained
- 1 can (8 ounces) tomato sauce
- 1 cup water
- 2 to 3 tablespoons chili powder
- 2 garlic cloves, minced
- ½ teaspoon ground cumin
- ⅛ to ¼ teaspoon cayenne pepper
- ¾ cup shredded reduced-fat cheddar cheese

1. Place bulgur in a large bowl; stir in boiling water. Cover and let stand for 30 minutes or until most of the liquid is absorbed. Drain and squeeze dry.
2. In a large saucepan, saute green peppers and onion in oil until tender. Stir in the bulgur, tomato juice, beans, tomatoes, tomato sauce, water, chili powder, garlic, cumin and cayenne. Bring to a boil. Reduce heat; cover and simmer for 20-25 minutes or until heated through. Sprinkle with cheese.

Yellow Pepper Soup

Flavoring a soup with yellow peppers is an unexpected surprise. I'll occasionally include garlic and minced chives, too.
—EDWARD GRIFFITHS STOWE, VT

PREP: 20 MIN. • **COOK:** 40 MIN.
MAKES: 5 SERVINGS

- 2½ cups water
- 3 large sweet yellow peppers, chopped
- 1 large potato, chopped
- 1 large onion, chopped
- 3 garlic cloves, minced
- 1½ teaspoons sugar
- ¾ teaspoon salt
- ¼ teaspoon pepper
- 1 tablespoon butter
- 1 tablespoon olive oil
- 1 tablespoon minced chives

1. In a large saucepan, combine the first eight ingredients. Bring to a boil. Reduce heat; cover and simmer for 30 minutes or until vegetables are tender. Cool slightly.
2. In a blender, process soup in batches until smooth. Return mixture to the pan.
3. Add butter and oil; cook and stir until heated through and butter is melted (do not boil). Sprinkle with chives.

Caribbean Fruit Soup

Jerk seasoning with six fresh fruits in a soup recipe may seem odd, but you'll be convinced with the first spoonful.

—CHERYL PERRY HERTFORD, NC

PREP: 35 MIN. + CHILLING
MAKES: 12 SERVINGS (2 QUARTS)

- 1 cup each chopped peeled fresh peaches, nectarines, papaya and mango
- 1 cup chopped fresh pineapple
- 1 cup diced cantaloupe
- 1 cup chopped seeded peeled cucumber
- 1 cup chopped sweet red pepper
- ¼ cup thinly sliced green onions
- 2 cups frozen non-alcoholic pina colada mix, thawed
- 1 cup passion fruit or mango nectar
- ¼ cup minced fresh cilantro
- 2 tablespoons plus 2 teaspoons lime juice, divided
- 1 tablespoon sugar
- 1 tablespoon Caribbean jerk seasoning
- 1 teaspoon salt
- 1 teaspoon grated fresh gingerroot
- 1 teaspoon minced seeded jalapeno pepper
- 2 medium bananas, sliced
- 1 cup flaked coconut

1. In a large bowl, combine the peaches, nectarines, papaya, mango, pineapple, cantaloupe, cucumber, red pepper and onions. In a blender or food processor, place half the fruit mixture; cover and process until smooth.

2. Transfer to a large bowl; stir in the remaining fruit mixture, pina colada mix, nectar, cilantro, 2 tablespoons lime juice, sugar, jerk seasoning, salt, ginger and jalapeno. Cover and refrigerate for 3 hours or until chilled.
3. Toss bananas with remaining lime juice. Garnish soup with bananas and coconut.

Hearty Potato Soup

I grew up on a dairy farm in Holland, and now I love my life in Idaho's "potato country." My favorite potato soup originally called for heavy cream and bacon fat, but I've trimmed down the recipe.

—GLADYS DE BOER CASTLEFORD, ID

PREP: 10 MIN. • **COOK:** 30 MIN.
MAKES: 8-10 SERVINGS (ABOUT 2½ QUARTS)

- 6 medium potatoes, peeled and sliced
- 2 carrots, chopped
- 6 celery ribs, chopped
- 8 cups water
- 1 onion, chopped
- 6 tablespoons butter, cubed
- 6 tablespoons all-purpose flour
- 1 teaspoon salt
- ½ teaspoon pepper
- 1½ cups 2% milk

1. In a Dutch oven, cook the potatoes, carrots and celery in water until tender, about 15-20 minutes. Drain, reserving liquid and setting vegetables aside.
2. In the same pan, saute onion in butter until tender. Stir in the flour, salt and pepper; gradually add milk. Bring to a boil; cook and stir for 2 minutes or until thickened. Gently stir in cooked vegetables. Add 1 cup or more of reserved cooking liquid until soup is desired consistency.

HEARTY POTATO SOUP

Slow Cooker

75 65 70

When you're busy and just need a **set-it-and-forget-it** kind of meal, look no further than this helpful chapter. With **more than 30 recipes** to choose from, you can't go wrong. Let your slow cooker do all the work in the morning, then gather your loved ones around the kitchen table later to enjoy the finished result. **It's that easy!**

SPLIT PEA AND SAUSAGE SOUP

Split Pea and Sausage Soup

PREP: 25 MIN. • **COOK:** 7 HOURS
MAKES: 6 SERVINGS (2¼ QUARTS)

- 1 **pound smoked sausage, sliced**
- 1 **medium potato, peeled and cubed**
- 2 **medium carrots, thinly sliced**
- 2 **celery ribs, thinly sliced**
- 1 **medium onion, chopped**
- 2 **tablespoons butter**
- 3 **garlic cloves, minced**
- ¼ **teaspoon dried oregano**
- 1 **cup dried green split peas**
- 2½ **teaspoons chicken bouillon granules**
- 1 **bay leaf**
- 5 **cups water**

1. Saute the sausage, potato, carrots, celery and onion in butter in a large skillet until vegetables are crisp-tender. Add garlic and oregano; cook 2 minutes longer.
2. Transfer to a 5-qt. slow cooker. Add the peas, bouillon, bay leaf and water. Cover and cook on low for 7-8 hours or until peas are tender. Discard bay leaf.

Gyro Soup

If you're a fan of lamb, don't pass up this Greek-style soup. Seasoned with mint, rosemary and marjoram, it will transport you straight to the Mediterranean!

—**BRIDGET KLUSMAN** OTSEGO, MI

PREP: 25 MIN. • **COOK:** 6 HOURS
MAKES: 6 SERVINGS

- 2 **pounds ground lamb**
- 5 **cups water**
- 1 **can (14½ ounces) diced tomatoes, undrained**
- 1 **medium onion, chopped**
- ¼ **cup red wine**
- 3 **tablespoons minced fresh mint or 1 tablespoon dried mint**
- 6 **garlic cloves, minced**
- 1 **tablespoon dried marjoram**
- 1 **tablespoon dried rosemary, crushed**
- 2 **teaspoons salt**
- ½ **teaspoon pepper**
  Optional toppings: plain Greek yogurt and crumbled feta cheese

1. In a large skillet, cook lamb until no longer pink; drain. Transfer to a 4- or 5-qt. slow cooker. Add the water, tomatoes, onion, wine, mint, garlic, marjoram, rosemary, salt and pepper. Cover and cook on low for 6-8 hours or until flavors are blended.
2. Serve with yogurt and feta cheese if desired.

Hearty Beef & Bean Chili

Perfect for entertaining, this slow-cooker chili is ready to go after a little prep and a few hours of simmering. You'll have plenty of time to tend to other matters...and to greet guests!

—**JAN WAGNER-CUDA** DEER PARK, WA

PREP: 25 MIN. • **COOK:** 6 HOURS
MAKES: 14 SERVINGS (3½ QUARTS)

- 2 **pounds ground beef**
- 6 **cans (16 ounces each) hot chili beans, undrained**
- 1 **can (10 ounces) diced tomatoes and green chilies, undrained**
- 1 **can (8 ounces) tomato sauce**
- ¼ **cup chopped onion**
- 2 **tablespoons molasses**
- 1 **teaspoon salt-free Southwest chipotle seasoning blend**
- 1 **teaspoon Worcestershire sauce**
- ½ **teaspoon salt**
- ½ **teaspoon ground cumin**
- ½ **teaspoon chili powder**

1. In a large skillet, cook beef over medium heat until no longer pink; drain. Transfer to a 6-qt. slow cooker.
2. Stir in the remaining ingredients. Cover and cook on low for 6-8 hours or until heated through.

SPICY TURKEY KIELBASA SOUP

Spicy Turkey Kielbasa Soup

Should you have any left over, this soup is great reheated—all the ingredients get the chance to meld together. I like to serve steaming bowls of it with slices of rye bread.

—CAROL CUSTER CLIFTON PARK, NY

PREP: 15 MIN. • **COOK:** 8 HOURS
MAKES: 5 SERVINGS

- ½ **pound reduced-fat smoked turkey kielbasa, sliced**
- 1 **medium onion, chopped**
- 1 **medium green pepper, chopped**
- 1 **celery rib with leaves, thinly sliced**
- 4 **garlic cloves, minced**
- 2 **cans (14½ ounces each) reduced-sodium chicken broth**
- 1 **can (15½ ounces) great northern beans, rinsed and drained**
- 1 **can (14½ ounces) stewed tomatoes, cut up**
- 1 **small zucchini, sliced**
- 1 **medium carrot, shredded**
- 1 **tablespoon dried parsley flakes**
- ¼ **teaspoon crushed red pepper flakes**
- ¼ **teaspoon pepper**

1. In a nonstick skillet, cook kielbasa over medium heat until lightly browned. Add the onion, green pepper and celery; cook and stir for 3 minutes. Add garlic; cook 1 minute longer.
2. Transfer to a 5-qt. slow cooker. Stir in the remaining ingredients. Cover and cook on low for 8-9 hours.

You can freeze zucchini and **add it to soup** still frozen, but it should be thawed and patted dry for recipes such as breads or cakes.

Southwest Vegetarian Lentil Soup

Even the most devoted meat lovers won't miss it in this zippy dish. It's a variation of a chicken and lentil soup that I make for my vegan friends, but it seems to be a popular recipe with everyone.

—**LAURIE STOUT-LETZ** BOUNTIFUL, UT

PREP: 25 MIN. • **COOK:** 7 HOURS
MAKES: 6 SERVINGS (2 QUARTS)

- 3 **cups vegetable broth**
- 1 **large onion, chopped**
- 1 **can (10 ounces) mild diced tomatoes and green chilies, undrained**
- 1 **cup mild salsa**
- 1 **cup dried lentils, rinsed**
- 1 **cup frozen corn**
- 1 **can (8 ounces) tomato sauce**
- 1 **can (4 ounces) chopped green chilies**
- 3 **garlic cloves, minced**
- 1½ **teaspoons chili powder**
- 1 **teaspoon ground cumin**
- ½ **teaspoon celery salt**
- ½ **teaspoon paprika**
- ⅛ **teaspoon cayenne pepper**
- 1 **package (16 ounces) firm tofu, drained and cut into ¼-inch cubes**
- 1 **can (4¼ ounces) chopped ripe olives**
- 3 **green onions, sliced**

In a 3- or 4-qt. slow cooker, combine the first 14 ingredients. Cover and cook on low for 7-10 hours or until lentils are tender. Sprinkle with tofu, olives and green onions.

Butternut Squash Soup

The golden color, smooth texture and wonderful taste of this soup make it ideal for whenever you need a pick-me-up. It has a slight tang from the cream cheese, and the cinnamon adds a touch of spice. You'll love it!

—**JACKIE CAMPBELL** STANHOPE, NJ

PREP: 30 MIN. • **COOK:** 6¼ HOURS
MAKES: 14 SERVINGS (2½ QUARTS)

- 1 **medium onion, chopped**
- 2 **tablespoons butter**
- 1 **medium butternut squash (about 4 pounds), peeled and cubed**
- 3 **cans (14½ ounces each) vegetable broth**
- 1 **tablespoon brown sugar**
- 1 **tablespoon minced fresh gingerroot**
- 1 **garlic clove, minced**
- 1 **cinnamon stick (3 inches)**
- 1 **package (8 ounces) cream cheese, softened and cubed**

1. In a small skillet, saute onion in butter until tender. Transfer to a 5-or 6-qt. slow cooker; add squash. Combine the broth, brown sugar, ginger, garlic and cinnamon stick; pour over squash. Cover and cook on low for 6-8 hours or until squash is tender.

2. Cool slightly. Discard cinnamon stick. In a blender, process soup in batches until smooth. Return all to slow cooker. Whisk in cream cheese; cover and cook 15 minutes longer or until cheese is melted.

BUTTERNUT SQUASH SOUP

Lemon Chicken & Rice Soup

When buying chicken for this soup, take it to the butcher counter and ask the butcher to cube it for you. It will save you time and make your prep work a bit easier.

—**KRISTIN CHERRY** BOTHELL, WA

PREP: 35 MIN. • **COOK:** 4¼ HOURS
MAKES: 12 SERVINGS (4 QUARTS)

- 2 **tablespoons olive oil**
- 2 **pounds boneless skinless chicken breasts, cut into ½-inch pieces**
- 5 **cans (14½ ounces each) reduced-sodium chicken broth**
- 8 **cups coarsely chopped Swiss chard, kale or spinach**
- 2 **large carrots, finely chopped**
- 1 **small onion, chopped**
- 1 **medium lemon, halved and thinly sliced**
- ¼ **cup lemon juice**
- 4 **teaspoons grated lemon peel**
- ½ **teaspoon pepper**
- 4 **cups cooked brown rice**

1. In a large skillet, heat 1 tablespoon oil over medium-high heat. Add half of the chicken; cook and stir until browned. Transfer to a 6-qt. slow cooker. Repeat with remaining oil and chicken.

2. Stir broth, vegetables, lemon slices, lemon juice, lemon peel and pepper into chicken. Cook, covered, on low 4-5 hours or until chicken is tender. Stir in rice; heat through.

My husband and I used to own a pizzeria, where this dish was always popular. We've since sold the restaurant, but I still make the soup for potlucks and other gatherings.

—**ESTELLA PETERSON** MADRAS, OR

PEPPERONI PIZZA SOUP

Pepperoni Pizza Soup

PREP: 20 MIN. • **COOK:** 8¼ HOURS
MAKES: 6 SERVINGS (2¼ QUARTS)

- 2 **cans (14½ ounces each) Italian stewed tomatoes, undrained**
- 2 **cans (14½ ounces each) reduced-sodium beef broth**
- 1 **small onion, chopped**
- 1 **small green pepper, chopped**
- ½ **cup sliced fresh mushrooms**
- ½ **cup sliced pepperoni, halved**
- 1½ **teaspoons dried oregano**
- ⅛ **teaspoon pepper**
- 1 **package (9 ounces) refrigerated cheese ravioli**
  Shredded part-skim mozzarella cheese and sliced ripe olives

1. In a 4-qt. slow cooker, combine the first eight ingredients. Cook, covered, on low 8-9 hours.

2. Stir in ravioli; cook, covered, on low 15-30 minutes or until pasta is tender. Top servings with cheese and olives.

Red Bean Vegetable Soup

Adding Cajun seasoning boosts the flavor of my bean soup, which is loaded with fresh vegetables.

—**RONNIE LAPPE** BROWNWOOD, TX

PREP: 15 MIN. • **COOK:** 6 HOURS
MAKES: 12 SERVINGS (3 QUARTS)

- 3 **large sweet red peppers, chopped**
- 3 **celery ribs, chopped**
- 2 **medium onions, chopped**
- 4 **cans (16 ounces each) kidney beans, rinsed and drained**
- 4 **cups chicken broth**
- 2 **bay leaves**
- ½ **to 1 teaspoon salt**
- ½ **to 1 teaspoon Cajun seasoning**
- ½ **teaspoon pepper**
- ¼ **to ½ teaspoon hot pepper sauce**

In a 5-qt. slow cooker, combine the peppers, celery, onions and beans. Stir in the remaining ingredients. Cover and cook on low for 6 hours or until vegetables are tender. Discard bay leaves before serving.

Autumn Pumpkin Chili

Even the most finicky of my grandchildren love this chili. Though it's especially good during the crisp days of fall, it's a year-round kind of recipe.

—KIMBERLY NAGY PORT HADLOCK, WA

PREP: 20 MIN. • **COOK:** 7 HOURS
MAKES: 4 SERVINGS

- 1 medium onion, chopped
- 1 small green pepper, chopped
- 1 small sweet yellow pepper, chopped
- 1 tablespoon canola oil
- 1 garlic clove, minced
- 1 pound ground turkey
- 1 can (15 ounces) solid-pack pumpkin
- 1 can (14½ ounces) diced tomatoes, undrained
- 4½ teaspoons chili powder
- ¼ teaspoon pepper
- ⅛ teaspoon salt
  Optional toppings: shredded cheddar cheese, sour cream and sliced green onions

1. Saute the onion and green and yellow peppers in oil in a large skillet until tender. Add garlic; cook 1 minute longer. Crumble turkey into skillet. Cook over medium heat until meat is no longer pink.
2. Transfer to a 3-qt. slow cooker. Stir in the pumpkin, tomatoes, chili powder, pepper and salt. Cover and cook on low for 7-9 hours. Serve with toppings of your choice.

Curried Ham & Split Pea Soup

Stock your freezer with portions of this classic soup with a twist. The curry gives it a punch and goes nicely with the salty ham.

—TRISHA KRUSE EAGLE, ID

PREP: 10 MIN. • **COOK:** 7 HOURS
MAKES: 8 SERVINGS (2 QUARTS)

- 2 tablespoons butter
- 1 medium onion, chopped
- 4 garlic cloves, minced
- 3 teaspoons curry powder
- 1 package (16 ounces) dried green split peas
- 2 cups cubed fully cooked ham
- 1 cup sliced fresh carrots
- 4 cups reduced-sodium beef broth
- 2 cups water
- ½ teaspoon pepper

1. In a skillet, heat butter over medium heat. Add onion; cook and stir 3-4 minutes or until tender. Add garlic and curry powder; cook 1 minute longer.
2. Transfer to a 4- or 5-qt. slow cooker. Add the remaining ingredients. Cook, covered, on low 7-9 hours or until the peas are tender. Stir before serving.

AUTUMN PUMPKIN CHILI

Colorful Minestrone

What makes my minestrone different from others? Butternut squash, a leek and fresh kale! Give it a try.

—TIFFANY ANDERSON-TAYLOR

GULFPORT, FL

PREP: 40 MIN. • **COOK:** 7½ HOURS
MAKES: 10 SERVINGS (3½ QUARTS)

- 1 medium leek (white portion only), thinly sliced
- 1 small onion, chopped
- 1 tablespoon olive oil
- 3 slices deli ham, chopped
- 2 garlic cloves, minced
- 2 quarts water
- 1 can (28 ounces) diced tomatoes, undrained
- 1 medium butternut squash, peeled, seeded and cubed
- 2 medium carrots, coarsely chopped
- 2 celery ribs, chopped
- 2 cups fresh baby spinach, cut into thin strips
- 1 cup fresh kale, trimmed and cut into thin strips
- 1 medium potato, peeled and cubed
- 1 tablespoon minced fresh rosemary
- 1 teaspoon salt
  Pepper to taste
- 1 can (15 ounces) white kidney or cannellini beans, rinsed and drained

1. In a small skillet, saute leek and onion in oil for 2 minutes or until vegetables are tender. Add ham and garlic; cook 1 minute longer.
2. Transfer ham mixture to a 5-qt. slow cooker. Stir in the water, vegetables, rosemary, salt and pepper. Cover and cook on low for 7-8 hours or until vegetables are tender.
3. Stir in beans; cover and cook 30 minutes longer.

This easy chili is loaded up with lots of chicken and beans. If you need to tone down the heat, dab on a spoonful of cool sour cream.

—FRED LOCKWOOD PLANO, TX

Green Chile Chicken Chili

PREP: 25 MIN. • **COOK:** 5 HOURS
MAKES: 10 SERVINGS (3½ QUARTS)

- 4 bone-in chicken breast halves (14 ounces each)
- 2 medium onions, chopped
- 2 medium green peppers, chopped
- 1 cup pickled jalapeno slices
- 1 can (4 ounces) chopped green chilies
- 2 jars (16 ounces each) salsa verde
- 2 cans (15½ ounces each) navy beans, rinsed and drained
- 1 cup (8 ounces) sour cream
- ½ cup minced fresh cilantro
  Optional toppings: shredded Colby-Monterey Jack cheese, additional sour cream and crushed tortilla chips

1. Place the chicken, onions, peppers, jalapenos and chilies in a 5- or 6-qt. slow cooker. Pour salsa over top. Cover and cook on low for 5-6 hours or until chicken is tender.
2. Remove chicken; cool slightly. Shred chicken with two forks, discarding skin and bones; return meat to slow cooker. Stir in the beans, sour cream and cilantro; heat through. Serve with toppings of your choice.
NOTE *Wear disposable gloves when cutting hot peppers; the oils can burn skin. Avoid touching your face.*

GREEN CHILE CHICKEN CHILI

Southwest Beef Stew

I made this stew for my ladies' group at church, and it was a big hit. Best of all, I could start the soup before I left for work in the morning and have it ready to go by the time I got home.

—ANITA ROBERSON WILLIAMSTON, NC

PREP: 30 MIN. • **COOK:** 7 HOURS
MAKES: 11 SERVINGS (2¾ QUARTS)

- 1½ pounds lean ground beef (90% lean)
- 1 large onion, chopped
- 2 cans (14½ ounces each) diced tomatoes, undrained
- 1 package (16 ounces) frozen corn
- 1 can (15 ounces) black beans, rinsed and drained
- 1 can (14½ ounces) chicken broth
- 1 can (10 ounces) diced tomatoes and green chilies, undrained
- 1 teaspoon garlic powder
- 1½ teaspoons salt-free Southwest chipotle seasoning blend
- 1½ cups cooked rice
- ¼ cup shredded cheddar cheese

1. In a large skillet, cook beef and onion over medium heat until meat is no longer pink; drain.
2. Transfer to a 5-qt. slow cooker. Stir in tomatoes, corn, black beans, broth, tomatoes, garlic powder and seasoning blend. Cover and cook on low for 6-8 hours or until heated through.
3. Stir in rice; heat through. Sprinkle each serving with cheese.

Herbed Chicken & Spinach Soup

To create a hearty meal, I serve this substantial chicken soup with a side of crusty bread slathered in butter.

—TANYA MACDONALD
ANTIGONISH COUNTY, NS

PREP: 20 MIN. • **COOK:** 4½ HOURS
MAKES: 4 SERVINGS

- 1 pound boneless skinless chicken thighs, cut into ½-inch pieces
- 1 can (16 ounces) kidney beans, rinsed and drained
- 1 can (14½ ounces) chicken broth
- 1 medium onion, chopped
- 1 medium sweet red pepper, chopped
- 1 celery rib, chopped
- 2 tablespoons tomato paste
- 3 garlic cloves, minced
- ½ teaspoon minced fresh rosemary or ¼ teaspoon dried rosemary, crushed
- ½ teaspoon minced fresh thyme or ¼ teaspoon dried thyme
- ½ teaspoon dried oregano
- ¼ teaspoon salt
- ¼ teaspoon pepper
- 3 cups fresh baby spinach
- ¼ cup shredded Parmesan cheese

In a 3-qt. slow cooker, combine the first 13 ingredients. Cover and cook on low for 4-5 hours or until chicken is tender. Stir in spinach; cook 30 minutes longer or until spinach is wilted. Top with cheese.

Remove the leaves from either **fresh rosemary or thyme** easily. Hold the top of the sprig and strip downward (against the grain) to **collect the leaves.**

CHICKEN CASSOULET SOUP

1 can (14½ ounces) diced tomatoes, undrained
2 celery ribs, chopped
1 cup sliced fresh or frozen okra
1 medium onion, chopped
2 teaspoons Cajun seasoning
1 pound smoked kielbasa or Polish sausage, cut into 1-inch pieces

In a 5-qt. slow cooker, combine the first eight ingredients. Cover and cook on low for 6-8 hours or until the vegetables are tender. Stir in kielbasa. Cover and cook 30 minutes longer or until heated through.

Loaded Baked Potato Soup

The only thing that beats this comforting potato soup? The fact that it simmers on its own all day.

—BARBARA BLEIGH COLONIAL HEIGHTS, VA

PREP: 35 MIN. • **COOK:** 6 HOURS
MAKES: 10 SERVINGS

2 large onions, chopped
3 tablespoons butter
2 tablespoons all-purpose flour
2 cups water, divided
4 cups chicken broth
2 medium potatoes, peeled and diced
1½ cups mashed potato flakes
½ pound sliced bacon, cooked and crumbled
¾ teaspoon pepper
½ teaspoon salt
½ teaspoon dried basil
⅛ teaspoon dried thyme
1 cup half-and-half cream
½ cup shredded cheddar cheese
2 green onions, sliced

1. In a large skillet, saute onions in butter until tender. Stir in flour. Gradually stir in 1 cup water. Bring to a boil; cook and stir for 2 minutes or until thickened. Transfer to a 5-qt. slow cooker.
2. Add the broth, potatoes, potato flakes, bacon, pepper, salt, basil, thyme and remaining water. Cover and cook on low for 6-8 hours or until potatoes are tender. Stir in cream; heat through. Garnish with cheese and green onions.

Chicken Cassoulet Soup

After my sister spent a year in France as an au pair, I created this much simpler version of French cassoulet to welcome her home. It uses chicken instead of the usual duck.

—BRIDGET KLUSMAN OTSEGO, MI

PREP: 35 MIN. • **COOK:** 6 HOURS
MAKES: 7 SERVINGS (2¾ QUARTS)

½ pound bulk pork sausage
5 cups water
½ pound cubed cooked chicken
1 can (16 ounces) kidney beans, rinsed and drained
1 can (15 ounces) black beans, rinsed and drained
1 can (15 ounces) garbanzo beans or chickpeas, rinsed and drained
2 medium carrots, shredded
1 medium onion, chopped
¼ cup dry vermouth or chicken broth
5 teaspoons chicken bouillon granules
4 garlic cloves, minced
1 teaspoon dried lavender flowers, optional
½ teaspoon dried thyme
¼ teaspoon fennel seed, crushed
½ pound bacon strips, cooked and crumbled

1. In a large skillet, cook sausage over medium heat until no longer pink; drain.
2. Transfer to a 4- or 5-qt. slow cooker. Add the water, chicken, beans, carrots, onion, vermouth, bouillon, garlic, lavender if desired, thyme and fennel. Cover and cook on low for 6-8 hours or until heated through.
3. Divide among bowls; sprinkle with bacon.
NOTE *Look for dried lavender flowers in spice shops. If using lavender from the garden, make sure it hasn't been treated with chemicals.*

Zesty Garbanzo Sausage Soup

Even the busiest home cooks have time to prepare this Cajun-inspired soup. If your family prefers more spice, use medium salsa instead of mild.

—PRISCILLA DOYLE LUTZ, FL

PREP: 20 MIN. • **COOK:** 6½ HOURS
MAKES: 7 SERVINGS

2 cans (15 ounces each) garbanzo beans or chickpeas, rinsed and drained
3 cups water
1 jar (16 ounces) mild salsa

LOADED BAKED POTATO SOUP

Potato and Leek Soup

Full of veggies and bacon with just a little tanginess from sour cream, bowls of this soothing soup taste just as terrific with a sandwich as they do with crackers!

—**MELANIE WOODEN** RENO, NV

PREP: 20 MIN. • **COOK:** 8 HOURS
MAKES: 8 SERVINGS (2 QUARTS)

- 4 **cups chicken broth**
- 3 **medium potatoes, peeled and cubed**
- 1½ **cups chopped cabbage**
- 2 **medium carrots, chopped**
- 1 **medium leek (white portion only), chopped**
- 1 **medium onion, chopped**
- ¼ **cup minced fresh parsley**
- ½ **teaspoon salt**
- ½ **teaspoon caraway seeds**
- ½ **teaspoon pepper**
- 1 **bay leaf**
- ½ **cup sour cream**
- 1 **pound bacon strips, cooked and crumbled**

1. Combine the first 11 ingredients in a 4- or 5-qt. slow cooker. Cover and cook on low for 8-10 hours or until vegetables are tender.
2. Before serving, combine sour cream with 1 cup soup; return all to the slow cooker. Stir in bacon and discard bay leaf.

Sausage Pumpkin Soup

Here, wintery spices complement pumpkin and sausage for a uniquely tasty soup. Maple syrup imparts just the right amount of sweetness.

—**LEAH CREMENT** COLLEGE STATION, TX

PREP: 20 MIN. • **COOK:** 3 HOURS 10 MIN.
MAKES: 8 SERVINGS (2 QUARTS)

- 1 **pound bulk pork sausage**
- ⅓ **cup chopped onion**
- 2 **cans (14½ ounces each) chicken broth**
- 1 **can (15 ounces) solid-pack pumpkin**
- ½ **cup maple syrup**
- 1 **teaspoon pumpkin pie spice**
- ½ **teaspoon garlic powder**
- ¼ **teaspoon ground nutmeg**
- 1 **can (12 ounces) evaporated milk**

1. In a large skillet, cook sausage and onion until sausage is no longer pink; drain.
2. Transfer to a 4-qt. slow cooker. Add the broth, pumpkin, syrup, pie spice, garlic powder and nutmeg. Cover and cook on low for 3-4 hours or until flavors are blended. Stir in milk; heat through.

Mushroom Barley Soup

Like most other soups, this mushroom recipe tastes especially good with a thick slice of bread on the side for dunking.

—**CONSTANCE SULLIVAN** OCEANSIDE, CA

PREP: 25 MIN. + SOAKING • **COOK:** 5 HOURS
MAKES: 12 SERVINGS (3 QUARTS)

- ½ **cup dried great northern beans**
- 1 **pound sliced fresh mushrooms**
- 2 **cups chopped onions**
- 1 **medium leek (white portion only), sliced**
- 2 **tablespoons butter**
- 1 **to 2 garlic cloves, minced**
- 2 **cartons (32 ounces each) chicken broth**
- 3 **celery ribs, thinly sliced**
- 3 **large carrots, chopped**
- ½ **cup medium pearl barley**
- 2 **teaspoons dried parsley flakes**
- 1½ **teaspoons salt**
- 1 **bay leaf**
- ¼ **teaspoon white pepper**

1. Soak beans according to package directions. In a large skillet, cook the mushrooms, onions and leek in butter over medium heat until tender. Add garlic; cook 1 minute longer.
2. Transfer to a 6-qt. slow cooker. Drain and rinse beans, discarding liquid. Add the beans, broth, celery, carrots, barley, parsley, salt, bay leaf and pepper. Cover and cook on low for 5-6 hours or until beans and vegetables are tender. Discard bay leaf.

MUSHROOM BARLEY SOUP

Slow Cooker Pasta e Fagioli

I absolutely love making this soup. I have served it to many guests and it always seems to bring in compliments.

—PENNY NOVY BUFFALO GROVE, IL

PREP: 30 MIN. • **COOK:** 7½ HOURS
MAKES: 8 SERVINGS (2½ QUARTS)

- 1 **pound ground beef**
- 1 **medium onion, chopped**
- 1 **carton (32 ounces) chicken broth**
- 2 **cans (14½ ounces each) diced tomatoes, undrained**
- 1 **can (15 ounces) white kidney or cannellini beans, rinsed and drained**
- 2 **medium carrots, chopped**
- 1½ **cups finely chopped cabbage**
- 1 **celery rib, chopped**
- 2 **tablespoons minced fresh basil or 2 teaspoons dried basil**
- 2 **garlic cloves, minced**
- ½ **teaspoon salt**
- ½ **teaspoon pepper**
- 1 **cup ditalini or other small pasta**
  Grated Parmesan cheese, optional

1. In a large skillet, cook beef and onion over medium heat until beef is no longer pink and onion is tender; drain.

2. Transfer to a 4- or 5-qt. slow cooker. Stir in the broth, tomatoes, beans, carrots, cabbage, celery, basil, garlic, salt and pepper. Cover and cook on low for 7-8 hours or until vegetables are tender.

3. Stir in pasta. Cover and cook on high 30 minutes longer or until pasta is tender. Sprinkle with Parmesan if desired.

Posole Verde

With fresh tomatillos, green chilies and hominy, this nutritious soup gives a nod to authentic Mexican fare. Family and friends frequently request it when they're invited over for dinner.

—GAYLE EHRENMAN WHITE PLAINS, NY

PREP: 30 MIN. • **COOK:** 7 HOURS
MAKES: 8 SERVINGS (3 QUARTS)

- 1 **pork tenderloin (1 pound), cubed**
- 1 **package (12 ounces) fully cooked spicy chicken sausage links, sliced**
- 8 **tomatillos, husks removed and cut into 1-inch pieces**
- 2 **cans (14 ounces each) hominy, rinsed and drained**
- 1 **can (16 ounces) kidney beans, rinsed and drained**
- 1 **can (14½ ounces) chicken broth**
- 3 **cans (4 ounces each) chopped green chilies**
- 1 **large red onion, quartered and sliced**
- 2 **tablespoons brown sugar**
- 3 **garlic cloves, minced**
- 1 **tablespoon ground cumin**
- 1 **tablespoon chili powder**
- 1 **teaspoon dried oregano**
  Minced fresh cilantro, optional

In a 6-qt. slow cooker, combine the first 13 ingredients. Cover and cook on low for 7-10 hours or until pork is tender. Sprinkle with cilantro if desired.

Cheesy Cauliflower Soup

If you prefer chunky soup, skip the blender step in the recipe and stir the cheese and cream into the slow cooker, then heat on high until the cheese is nice and melted.

—**SHERYL PUNTER** WOODSTOCK, ON

PREP: 25 MIN. • **COOK:** 5½ HOURS
MAKES: 9 SERVINGS (2¼ QUARTS)

- 1 large head cauliflower, broken into florets
- 2 celery ribs
- 2 large carrots
- 1 large green pepper
- 1 small sweet red pepper
- 1 medium red onion
- 4 cups chicken broth
- ½ teaspoon Worcestershire sauce
- ¼ teaspoon salt
- ⅛ teaspoon pepper
- 2 cups (8 ounces) shredded cheddar cheese
- 2 cups half-and-half cream

1. Place cauliflower in a 4-qt. slow cooker. Chop the celery, carrots, peppers and onion; add to slow cooker. Stir in broth, Worcestershire sauce, salt and pepper. Cover and cook on low for 5-6 hours or until vegetables are tender.

2. In a blender, process soup in batches until smooth. Return all to slow cooker; stir in cheese and cream. Cover and cook on high for 30 minutes or until cheese is melted.

Mango & Coconut Chicken Soup

PREP: 25 MIN. • **COOK:** 6 HOURS
MAKES: 6 SERVINGS

- 1 broiler/fryer chicken (3 to 4 pounds), skin removed and cut up
- 2 tablespoons canola oil
- 1 can (15 ounces) whole baby corn, drained
- 1 package (10 ounces) frozen chopped spinach, thawed
- 1 cup frozen shelled edamame, thawed
- 1 small sweet red pepper, chopped
- 1 can (13.66 ounces) light coconut milk
- ½ cup mango salsa
- 1 teaspoon minced fresh gingerroot
- 1 medium mango, peeled and chopped
- 2 tablespoons lime juice
- 2 green onions, chopped

1. In a large skillet, brown chicken in oil in batches. Transfer chicken and drippings to a 5-qt. slow cooker. Add the corn, spinach, edamame and pepper. In a small bowl, combine the coconut milk, salsa and ginger; pour over vegetables.

2. Cover and cook on low for 6-8 hours or until the chicken is tender. Remove chicken; cool slightly. When the chicken is cool enough to handle, remove meat from bones; cut or shred meat into bite-size pieces. Return meat to slow cooker.

3. Just before serving, stir in mango and lime juice. Sprinkle servings with green onions.

> I enjoy preparing dinner in a slow cooker because it's the definition of carefree cooking. This chicken dish uses ingredients that I love, such as coconut milk, edamame and fresh ginger. If you're heading to a party or potluck, bring this along.
>
> —**ROXANNE CHAN** ALBANY, CA

MANGO & COCONUT CHICKEN SOUP

ANYTHING GOES SAUSAGE SOUP

Lentil Stew

Sometimes you just need a break from the usual soup recipes, and this vegetarian stew is an ideal change. Adding the cream at the end gives it a smoother texture.

—**MICHELLE COLLINS** SUFFOLK, VA

PREP: 45 MIN. • **COOK:** 6 HOURS
MAKES: 8 SERVINGS (2¾ QUARTS)

- 2 **large onions, thinly sliced, divided**
- 2 **tablespoons canola oil**
- 2 **tablespoons minced fresh gingerroot**
- 3 **garlic cloves, minced**
- 8 **plum tomatoes, chopped**
- 2 **teaspoons ground coriander**
- 1½ **teaspoons ground cumin**
- ¼ **teaspoon cayenne pepper**
- 3 **cups vegetable broth**
- 2 **cups water**
- 2 **cups dried lentils, rinsed**
- 1 **can (4 ounces) chopped green chilies**
- ¾ **cup heavy whipping cream**
- 2 **tablespoons butter**
- 1 **teaspoon cumin seeds**
- 6 **cups hot cooked basmati or jasmine rice**
  Sliced green onions or minced fresh cilantro, optional

1. In a large skillet, saute half of the onions in oil until tender. Add ginger and garlic; saute for 1 minute. Add the tomatoes, coriander, cumin and cayenne pepper; cook and stir 5 minutes longer.

2. In a 4- or 5-qt. slow cooker, combine the vegetable broth, water, lentils, green chilies, tomato mixture and remaining onion. Cover and cook on low for 6-8 hours or until lentils are tender.

3. Just before serving, stir cream into slow cooker. In a small skillet, heat butter over medium heat. Add cumin seeds; cook and stir for 1-2 minutes or until golden brown. Add to lentil mixture.

4. To serve, spoon over rice. Sprinkle with green onions or cilantro if desired.

Anything Goes Sausage Soup

I call this recipe "anything goes" because you can add or take out ingredients as you wish, and the soup will still turn out absolutely delicious. It's impossible to have just one bowl, unless of course your first bowl is huge and filled to the brim!

—**SHEENA WELLARD** NAMPA, ID

PREP: 40 MIN. • **COOK:** 9½ HOURS
MAKES: 15 SERVINGS (ABOUT 4 QUARTS)

- 1 **pound bulk pork sausage**
- 4 **cups water**
- 1 **can (10¾ ounces) condensed cream of mushroom soup, undiluted**
- 1 **can (10¾ ounces) condensed cheddar cheese soup, undiluted**
- 5 **medium red potatoes, cubed**
- 4 **cups chopped cabbage**
- 3 **large carrots, thinly sliced**
- 4 **celery ribs, chopped**
- 1 **medium zucchini, chopped**
- 1 **large onion, chopped**
- 5 **chicken bouillon cubes**
- 1 **tablespoon dried parsley flakes**
- ¾ **teaspoon pepper**
- 1 **can (12 ounces) evaporated milk**

1. In a large skillet, cook sausage over medium heat until no longer pink; drain. Transfer to a 6-qt. slow cooker. Stir in the water and soups until blended. Add the vegetables, bouillon, parsley and pepper.

2. Cover and cook on low for 9-10 hours or until vegetables are tender. Stir in the milk; cover and cook 30 minutes longer.

SEAFOOD CIOPPINO

Seafood Cioppino

If you're looking for a great seafood recipe, give this fish stew a try. Clams, crab, haddock and shrimp make it fancy enough to serve for an elegant meal.
—**LISA MORIARTY** WILTON, NH

PREP: 20 MIN. • **COOK:** 4½ HOURS
MAKES: 8 SERVINGS (2½ QUARTS)

- 1 can (28 ounces) diced tomatoes, undrained
- 2 medium onions, chopped
- 3 celery ribs, chopped
- 1 bottle (8 ounces) clam juice
- 1 can (6 ounces) tomato paste
- ½ cup white wine or vegetable broth
- 5 garlic cloves, minced
- 1 tablespoon red wine vinegar
- 1 tablespoon olive oil
- 1 to 2 teaspoons Italian seasoning
- ½ teaspoon sugar
- 1 bay leaf
- 1 pound haddock fillets, cut into 1-inch pieces
- 1 pound uncooked small shrimp, peeled and deveined
- 1 can (6 ounces) lump crabmeat, drained
- 1 can (6 ounces) chopped clams
- 2 tablespoons minced fresh parsley or 2 teaspoons dried parsley flakes

In a 4- or 5-qt. slow cooker, combine the first 12 ingredients. Cover and cook on low for 4-5 hours. Stir in the haddock, shrimp, crabmeat and clams. Cover and cook 30 minutes longer or until fish flakes easily with a fork and shrimp turn pink. Stir in parsley. Discard bay leaf.

Navy Bean Vegetable Soup

My family really likes bean soup, so I came up with this enticing version. The leftovers are, dare I say, even better the next day.
—**ELEANOR MIELKE** MITCHELL, SD

PREP: 15 MIN. • **COOK:** 9 HOURS
MAKES: 12 SERVINGS (3 QUARTS)

- 4 medium carrots, thinly sliced
- 2 celery ribs, chopped
- 1 medium onion, chopped
- 2 cups cubed fully cooked ham
- 1½ cups dried navy beans

- 1 envelope vegetable recipe mix (Knorr)
- 1 envelope onion soup mix
- 1 bay leaf
- ½ teaspoon pepper
- 8 cups water

In a 5-qt. slow cooker, combine the first nine ingredients. Stir in water. Cover and cook on low for 9-10 hours or until beans are tender. Discard bay leaf.

Mulligatawny Soup

I learned to cook and bake from my mom and grandmother and always try to use fresh fruits, vegetables and herbs like they did. I can make this delicious, satisfying soup with leftover chicken, turkey and sometimes beef, pork or lamb.
—**MARY ANN MARINO** WEST PITTSBURGH, PA

PREP: 20 MIN. • **COOK:** 6 HOURS
MAKES: 8 SERVINGS (2 QUARTS)

- 1 carton (32 ounces) chicken broth
- 1 can (14½ ounces) diced tomatoes
- 2 cups cubed cooked chicken
- 1 large tart apple, peeled and chopped
- ¼ cup finely chopped onion
- ¼ cup chopped carrot
- ¼ cup chopped green pepper
- 1 tablespoon minced fresh parsley
- 2 teaspoons lemon juice
- 1 teaspoon salt
- 1 teaspoon curry powder
- ½ teaspoon sugar
- ¼ teaspoon pepper
- 2 whole cloves

In a 3- or 4-qt. slow cooker, combine all ingredients. Cover and cook on low for 6-8 hours or until vegetables are tender. Discard cloves.

Italian Shredded Pork Stew

Need a warm, soothing meal for a blustery night? Throw together this slow-cooked stew loaded with sweet potatoes and kale. And the shredded pork is oh-so-tender!

—**ROBIN JUNGERS** CAMPBELLSPORT, WI

PREP: 20 MIN. • **COOK:** 8 HOURS
MAKES: 9 SERVINGS (3½ QUARTS)

- 2 **medium sweet potatoes, peeled and cubed**
- 2 **cups chopped fresh kale**
- 1 **large onion, chopped**
- 3 **garlic cloves, minced**
- 1 **boneless pork shoulder butt roast (2½ to 3½ pounds)**
- 1 **can (14 ounces) white kidney or cannellini beans, rinsed and drained**
- 1½ **teaspoons Italian seasoning**
- ½ **teaspoon salt**
- ½ **teaspoon pepper**
- 3 **cans (14½ ounces each) chicken broth**
  Sour cream, optional

1. Place the sweet potatoes, kale, onion and garlic in a 5-qt. slow cooker. Place roast on vegetables. Add the beans and seasonings. Pour broth over top. Cover and cook on low for 8-10 hours or until meat is tender.
2. Remove meat; cool slightly. Skim fat from cooking juices. Shred pork with two forks and return to slow cooker; heat through. Garnish servings with sour cream if desired.

Spicy Chicken and Hominy Soup

Also known as "posole," this New Year's soup promises good luck. The recipe is popular in New Mexico, where I'm originally from. My take has a kick to it.

—**JANET CHRISTINE MCDANIEL**
ARLINGTON, TX

PREP: 15 MIN. • **COOK:** 4 HOURS
MAKES: 4 SERVINGS

- 1 **pound boneless skinless chicken breasts, cubed**
- 2 **tablespoons olive oil**
- 1 **medium onion, chopped**
- 3 **garlic cloves, minced**
- 2 **chipotle peppers in adobo sauce**
- 2 **cans (14½ ounces each) chicken broth, divided**

SPICY CHICKEN AND HOMINY SOUP

- 1 **can (15 ounces) hominy, rinsed and drained**
- 1 **can (4 ounces) chopped green chilies**
- 1 **teaspoon dried oregano**
- 1 **teaspoon ground cumin**
- ¼ **teaspoon pepper**

1. In a large skillet, brown chicken in oil. With a slotted spoon, transfer the chicken to a 3- or 4-qt. slow cooker. In the same skillet, saute onion and garlic in drippings until tender; add to chicken.
2. Place chipotle peppers and ¼ cup broth in a blender or food processor; cover and process until blended. Add to chicken mixture. Stir in the hominy, chilies, seasonings and remaining broth. Cover and cook on low for 4-5 hours or until chicken is tender.

Beef Barley Soup

Here's a soup that will certainly stick to your ribs. I've also used a chuck roast, rump roast and London broil that's been cut into bite-size pieces—each substitute was a tremendous success.

—**JANE MCMILLAN** DANIA BEACH, FL

PREP: 20 MIN. • **COOK:** 8½ HOURS
MAKES: 8 SERVINGS (2 QUARTS)

- 1½ **pounds beef stew meat, cut into ½-inch cubes**
- 1 **tablespoon canola oil**
- 1 **carton (32 ounces) beef broth**
- 1 **bottle (12 ounces) beer or nonalcoholic beer**
- 1 **small onion, chopped**
- ½ **cup medium pearl barley**
- 3 **garlic cloves, minced**
- 1 **teaspoon dried oregano**
- 1 **teaspoon dried parsley flakes**
- 1 **teaspoon Worcestershire sauce**
- ½ **teaspoon crushed red pepper flakes**
- ½ **teaspoon pepper**
- ¼ **teaspoon salt**
- 1 **bay leaf**
- 2 **cups frozen mixed vegetables, thawed**

1. In a large skillet, brown beef in oil; drain. Transfer to a 3-qt. slow cooker.
2. Add the broth, beer, onion, barley, garlic, oregano, parsley, Worcestershire sauce, pepper flakes, pepper, salt and bay leaf. Cover and cook on low for 8-10 hours.
3. Stir in vegetables; cover and cook 30 minutes longer or until meat is tender and vegetables are heated through. Discard bay leaf.

Cream Soups & Chowders

81   89   82

There's something **wonderfully comforting** about cream soups and chowders. With just a little work, these filling **all-time classics** make a welcomed addition to any menu. Liven up the dinner table tonight with any of the following **heartwarming favorites.** You won't believe how easy it is to **ladle out some love.**

CREAMY SPINACH & POTATO SOUP

Creamy Spinach & Potato Soup

My three boys love this recipe, and I even pack it in their school lunches occasionally. I sometimes add ham or sprinkle chopped bacon pieces on top.
—**AMY SAMUEL** NORTH POLE, AK

PREP: 25 MIN. • **COOK:** 20 MIN.
MAKES: 9 SERVINGS

- 6 cups cubed peeled potatoes
- 2 medium leeks (white portion only), chopped
- 2 tablespoons canola oil
- ½ cup all-purpose flour
- 1 teaspoon sodium-free chicken bouillon granules
- 3 cups reduced-sodium chicken broth
- 1 can (12 ounces) reduced-fat evaporated milk
- 1 package (9 ounces) fresh spinach, chopped
- ½ teaspoon salt
- ¼ teaspoon pepper
- ½ cup shredded cheddar cheese

1. Place potatoes in a large saucepan and cover with water. Bring to a boil. Reduce heat; cover and cook for 10-12 minutes or until tender. Drain. Mash 2 cups potatoes; set aside.

2. In a Dutch oven, saute leeks in oil until tender. Whisk the flour, bouillon granules and broth until smooth. Gradually stir into pan. Add milk. Bring to a boil; cook and stir for 2 minutes or until thickened.

3. Stir in mashed potatoes. Add spinach, salt, pepper and remaining potatoes; cook just until spinach is wilted. Sprinkle with cheese.

Quick Salmon Chowder

I made up this quick creamy chowder one winter afternoon. I like to use a can of sockeye salmon for the best flavor. The soup can also be seasoned with tarragon instead of dill.
—**TOM BAILEY** GOLDEN VALLEY, MN

START TO FINISH: 10 MIN.
MAKES: 7 SERVINGS

- 3 cans (10¾ ounces each) condensed cream of potato soup, undiluted
- 2⅔ cups half-and-half cream
- 1 can (14¾ ounces) salmon, drained, bones and skin removed
- 1 teaspoon dill weed
- ½ teaspoon salt
- ¼ teaspoon white pepper
- ¼ teaspoon crushed red pepper flakes

In a large saucepan, combine all of the ingredients. Cook and stir over medium heat until chowder is heated through.

(5)INGREDIENTS
Rivel Soup

For years, I'd been trying to figure out how my grandmother made her rivel soup. I was fascinated to discover that the recipe wasn't just something she came up with to feed her family. It's a treasured home-style soup, and many people have their own special version.
—**KATHY KEGLEY** RURAL RETREAT, VA

START TO FINISH: 10 MIN.
MAKES: 6 SERVINGS

- 1 cup all-purpose flour
- ½ teaspoon salt
- 1 egg
- 4 cups 2% milk
  Minced fresh parsley and coarsely ground pepper

1. In a small bowl, combine flour and salt. Cut in egg with a fork until crumbly.

2. In a large saucepan, heat milk over medium heat until bubbles form around sides of pan. Gradually add flour mixture; bring to a gentle boil, stirring constantly. Cook and stir for 1-2 minutes or until rivels are cooked through. Sprinkle servings with parsley and pepper.

Hearty Leek and Potato Soup

Talk about a winner! This soup transforms into a complete meal when served alongside dinner rolls fresh from the oven.

—**RACHEL TAYLOR** SPRINGFIELD, TN

PREP: 20 MIN. • **COOK:** 30 MIN.
MAKES: 8 SERVINGS (2 QUARTS)

- 3 **celery ribs, chopped**
- 2 **medium onions, chopped**
- 3 **medium leeks (white portion only), chopped**
- 1 **medium green pepper, chopped**
- 2 **jalapeno peppers, seeded and chopped**
- 6 **garlic cloves, minced**
- 2 **tablespoons olive oil**
- 4 **medium potatoes, peeled and cubed**
- 2 **cans (14½ ounces each) vegetable broth**
- 1 **cup water**
- ½ **teaspoon pepper**
- ¼ **teaspoon salt**
- 3 **tablespoons all-purpose flour**
- ¼ **cup fat-free milk**
- ½ **cup reduced-fat sour cream**
- 2 **green onions, chopped**

1. In a nonstick Dutch oven, saute the celery, onions, leeks, green pepper, jalapenos and garlic in oil until tender. Add the potatoes, broth, water, pepper and salt. Bring to a boil. Reduce heat; cover and simmer for 10-15 minutes or until potatoes are tender, stirring occasionally.

2. Combine flour and milk until smooth; stir into soup. Cook and stir for 2 minutes or until thickened and bubbly. Reduce heat to low. Stir in sour cream and green onions until blended; heat through (do not boil). **NOTE** *Wear disposable gloves when cutting hot peppers; the oils can burn skin. Avoid touching your face.*

Day After Easter Soup

Every spring I wait impatiently for the asparagus crop to arrive so I can make this soup. It gets its name from an Easter where I added extra asparagus to the pan.

—**SUSAN WILSON** MILWAUKEE, WI

PREP: 25 MIN. • **COOK:** 45 MIN.
MAKES: 9 SERVINGS (2¼ QUARTS)

- 2 **medium leeks (white portion only), chopped**
- 2 **tablespoons butter**
- 2 **tablespoons all-purpose flour**
- 1 **carton (32 ounces) vegetable broth**
- 1 **cup water**
- 1 **tablespoon minced fresh parsley**
- 1 **teaspoon herbes de Provence**
- 1 **teaspoon minced chives**
- ½ **teaspoon celery seed**
- ¼ **teaspoon ground nutmeg**
- 1 **pound fresh asparagus, trimmed**
- 5 **medium red potatoes, peeled and cut into ½-inch cubes**
- 1½ **cups cubed fully cooked lean ham**
- 1¼ **cups half-and-half cream**
- 3 **tablespoons shredded Gruyere or Swiss cheese**

1. In a large saucepan, saute leeks in butter until tender. Stir in flour until blended. Gradually add the broth, water, parsley, herbes de Provence, chives, celery seed and nutmeg. Bring to a boil; cook and stir for 2 minutes or until thickened.

2. Cut tips off asparagus and set aside. Cut stalks into ½-in. pieces; add to pan. Reduce heat; cover and simmer for 10-15 minutes or until asparagus is tender. Cool slightly.

3. In a blender, process soup in batches until smooth. Return all to pan. Stir in potatoes. Bring to a boil. Reduce heat; cover and simmer for 10 minutes. Stir in asparagus tips; cover and simmer 5-8 minutes longer or until vegetables are tender. Stir in ham and cream; heat through. Sprinkle with cheese. **NOTE** *Look for herbes de Provence in the spice aisle.*

DAY AFTER EASTER SOUP

PRISCILLA'S VEGETABLE CHOWDER

Priscilla's Vegetable Chowder

Take my chowder recipe to a fancy new level by serving it in a bread bowl. Your family will love it!

—JENNA JACKSON SALT LAKE CITY, UT

PREP: 25 MIN. • **COOK:** 30 MIN.
MAKES: 12 SERVINGS (3 QUARTS)

- 3 **cups diced peeled potatoes**
- 2½ **cups broccoli florets**
- 1 **cup chopped onion**
- 1 **cup grated carrots**
- 2 **celery ribs, diced**
- 4 **teaspoons chicken bouillon granules**
- 3 **cups water**
- ¾ **cup butter, cubed**
- ¾ **cup all-purpose flour**
- 4 **cups milk**
- 1 **teaspoon salt**
- ¼ **teaspoon pepper**
- 1 **cup cubed fully cooked ham**
- 1 **cup (4 ounces) shredded cheddar cheese**

1. In a Dutch oven, combine the potatoes, broccoli, onion, carrots, celery, bouillon and water; simmer for 20 minutes or until vegetables are tender.

2. In a large saucepan, melt butter; stir in flour. Cook and stir over medium heat for 2 minutes. Whisk in the milk, salt and pepper. Bring to a boil; cook and stir for 2 minutes or until thickened. Add to vegetable mixture with the ham; simmer 10 minutes until heated through. Stir in cheese just until melted.

Mushroom & Wild Rice Soup

You can tell how much I adore mushrooms just by looking at this recipe. I used four kinds of mushrooms!

—MARY MCVEY COLFAX, NC

PREP: 25 MIN. + STANDING • **COOK:** 45 MIN.
MAKES: 12 SERVINGS (2¼ QUARTS)

- 2½ **cups water**
- 1 **ounce dried porcini mushrooms**
- 1 **ounce dried shiitake mushrooms**
- 3 **tablespoons butter**
- 1 **small onion, diced**
- ½ **pound sliced fresh mushrooms**
- ½ **pound sliced baby portobello mushrooms**
- 3 **garlic cloves, minced**
- 4 **cups chicken broth**
- 1 **package (6 ounces) long grain and wild rice mix**
- ½ **teaspoon salt**
- ¼ **teaspoon white pepper**
- ½ **cup cold water**
- 4 **teaspoons cornstarch**
- 1 **cup heavy whipping cream**

1. In a small saucepan, bring water to a boil; add dried mushrooms. Remove from the heat; let stand for 25-30 minutes or until softened.

2. Using a slotted spoon, remove mushrooms; rinse. Trim and discard stems from shiitake mushrooms. Chop mushrooms. Strain soaking liquid through a fine-mesh strainer. Reserve mushrooms and soaking liquid.

3. In a Dutch oven, heat butter over medium-high heat. Add onion; cook and stir until tender. Add fresh and baby portobello mushrooms; cook and stir until tender. Add garlic; cook 1 minute longer.

4. Stir in the broth, rice mix with contents of seasoning packet, reserved dried mushrooms and soaking liquid, salt and pepper. Bring to a boil. Reduce heat; cover and simmer for 20-25 minutes or until rice is tender. In a small bowl, mix water and cornstarch until smooth; stir into soup. Bring to a boil; cook and stir for 2 minutes or until thickened. Stir in cream; heat through.

KNOEPHLA SOUP

Knoephla Soup

My mom would make this traditional German soup when I was growing up. Knoephla (pronounced nip-fla) soup is now a warm and comforting meal for my own family.

—**LORRAINE MEYERS** WILLOW CITY, ND

PREP: 20 MIN. • **COOK:** 40 MIN.
MAKES: 8-10 SERVINGS (2½ QUARTS)

½ cup butter, cubed
3 medium potatoes, peeled and cubed
1 small onion, grated
3 cups milk
6 cups water
6 teaspoons chicken or 3 vegetable bouillon cubes
KNOEPHLA
1½ cups all-purpose flour
1 egg, beaten
5 to 6 tablespoons milk
½ teaspoon salt
Minced fresh parsley, optional

1. In a large skillet, melt butter; cook potatoes and onion for 20-25 minutes or until tender. Add milk; heat through but do not boil. Set aside. In a Dutch oven, bring water and bouillon to a boil.
2. Meanwhile, combine first four knoephla ingredients to form a stiff dough. Roll into a ½-in. rope. Cut into ¼-in. pieces and drop into boiling broth. Reduce heat; cover and simmer for 10 minutes. Add the potato mixture; heat through. Sprinkle with parsley if desired.

Creamy Rutabaga Soup

I attended a dinner party where this smooth, nutty-tasting soup was served as an appetizer. No one guessed that rutabagas were the main ingredient!

—**CAPPY HALL REARICK** ST. SIMONS ISLAND, GA

PREP: 55 MIN. • **COOK:** 10 MIN.
MAKES: 10 SERVINGS (2½ QUARTS)

1 medium onion, chopped
1 celery rib, chopped
1 tablespoon butter
4 cups cubed peeled rutabagas (about 2 medium)
1½ cups uncooked long grain rice
1½ cups water
5½ cups chicken broth, divided
1¼ cups whole milk
½ teaspoon salt
¼ teaspoon pepper
Sour cream and minced fresh chives

1. In a Dutch oven, saute onion and celery in butter until tender. Add the rutabagas, rice, water and 2½ cups broth. Bring to a boil. Reduce heat; simmer, uncovered, for 25-35 minutes or until rutabagas are tender.
2. In a blender, cover and process soup in batches until smooth. Return all to the pan. Stir in the milk, salt, pepper and remaining broth; heat through (do not boil). Garnish servings with sour cream and chives.

Cream of Cauliflower Soup

This mildly cheesy cauliflower soup is a favorite of mine. I make it often in summer, although it's good any time.
—**KAREN BROWN** WEST LAFAYETTE, OH

START TO FINISH: 20 MIN.
MAKES: 6 SERVINGS

- ⅓ cup green onions (tops only)
- 2 tablespoons butter
- 2 tablespoons all-purpose flour
- ½ teaspoon salt
- 2 cups chicken broth
- 2¼ cups frozen cauliflower, thawed and chopped
- 2 cups 1% milk
- 1½ cups (6 ounces) shredded reduced-fat cheddar cheese
- 2 tablespoons dry sherry, optional
- 1 tablespoon minced chives

1. In a saucepan, saute onions in butter until tender. Stir in flour and salt until blended. Gradually add broth. Bring to a boil; cook and stir for 2 minutes or until thickened. Reduce heat.
2. Add cauliflower; simmer for 2 minutes. Add the milk and cheese; cook and stir until cheese is melted. Stir in sherry if desired. Garnish with chives.

Rustic Autumn Soup

This is the best of the fall season, in a bowl! The root vegetables really shine when combined with the subtle sweetness of apple.
—**GREG HAGELI** ELMHURST, IL

PREP: 30 MIN. • **COOK:** 25 MIN.
MAKES: 13 SERVINGS (3¼ QUARTS)

- 5 medium parsnips, chopped
- 5 medium carrots, chopped
- 2 medium onions, chopped
- 1 medium sweet potato, peeled and chopped
- 1 medium turnip, peeled and chopped
- ½ medium tart apple, peeled and chopped
- 2 tablespoons chopped roasted sweet red pepper
- 2 celery ribs, chopped
- 3 cans (14½ ounces each) reduced-sodium chicken broth
- 2 bay leaves
- 1 garlic clove, minced
- 1 teaspoon dried tarragon
- ½ teaspoon salt
- ½ teaspoon pepper
- 2 cups half-and-half cream
  Optional garnish: additional cooked finely chopped carrots, parsnips and/or apples, fresh chives

1. In a Dutch oven, combine the first 14 ingredients. Bring to a boil. Reduce heat; cover and simmer for 20-25 minutes or until tender. Discard bay leaves. Cool slightly.
2. In a blender, process soup in batches until smooth. Return all to the pan; add cream and heat through. If desired, garnish with additional cooked vegetables and/or apples and chives.

RUSTIC AUTUMN SOUP

SIMPLY ELEGANT TOMATO SOUP

Simply Elegant Tomato Soup

If you've only had tomato soup from a can, you're going to be blown away when you try this homemade version. It's velvety, creamy and oh-so-good!

—HEIDI BLANKEN SEDRO-WOOLLEY, WA

PREP: 25 MIN. • **COOK:** 20 MIN.
MAKES: 4 SERVINGS

- 4 **pounds tomatoes (about 10 medium)**
- 1 **tablespoon butter**
- 3 **tablespoons minced chives, divided**
- 1 **teaspoon salt**
- ½ **teaspoon pepper**
- 2 **cups half-and-half cream**

1. In a large saucepan, bring 8 cups water to a boil. Using a slotted spoon, place tomatoes, one at a time, in boiling water for 30-60 seconds. Remove each tomato and immediately plunge in ice water. Peel and quarter tomatoes; remove seeds.
2. In another large saucepan, melt butter. Add tomatoes, 2 tablespoons chives, salt and pepper. Bring to a boil. Reduce heat; simmer, uncovered, for 6-7 minutes or until tender, stirring occasionally. Remove from the heat. Cool slightly.

3. In a blender, process soup until blended. Return to the pan. Stir in cream; heat through. Sprinkle each serving with remaining chives.

Creamy Turnip Soup

This soup is served at a nearby fall festival. It reheats nicely in a slow cooker.

—LIZ WHEELER WILMINGTON, VT

PREP: 20 MIN. • **COOK:** 20 MIN.
MAKES: 9 SERVINGS (2¼ QUARTS)

- 2 **tablespoons butter**
- 1 **medium onion, chopped**
- 3 **garlic cloves, minced**
- ½ **cup white wine or reduced-sodium chicken broth**
- 3 **pounds turnips, peeled and cut into 1-inch cubes**
- 1 **carton (32 ounces) reduced-sodium chicken broth**
- 1 **medium potato, peeled and cubed**
- 1 **cup half-and-half cream**
- ½ **teaspoon salt**
- ½ **teaspoon ground nutmeg**
- ½ **teaspoon olive oil**
- 3 **cups fresh baby spinach**

1. In a Dutch oven, heat butter over medium-high heat. Add onion; cook and stir until tender. Add garlic; cook 1 minute longer. Stir in wine. Bring to a boil; cook until liquid is reduced by half.

2. Add turnips, broth and potato. Bring to a boil. Reduce heat; simmer, uncovered, 20-25 minutes or until vegetables are tender. Cool slightly.
3. In a food processor, process soup in batches until smooth. Return all to pan. Stir in cream, salt and nutmeg; heat through.
4. Meanwhile, in a large nonstick skillet, heat oil over medium-high heat. Add spinach; cook and stir just until wilted. Serve with soup.

Cheese Soup with a Twist

One of my favorite childhood memories is of my Aunt Claire serving up hearty bowlfuls of her famous cheesy soup. She would pair it with a slice of warm buttered bread for a down-home lunch. I love making it now to share.

—ROB FEEZOR ALEXANDRIA, VA

START TO FINISH: 30 MIN.
MAKES: 8 SERVINGS (2 QUARTS)

- 5 **bacon strips, diced**
- ½ **cup chopped celery**
- ½ **cup chopped onion**
- ½ **cup chopped green pepper**
- ¼ **cup all-purpose flour**
- ¼ **teaspoon coarsely ground pepper**
- 4 **cups reduced-sodium chicken broth**
- 2 **cups milk**
- 3 **cups cubed process cheese (Velveeta)**
- ½ **cup sliced pimiento-stuffed olives**
- ½ **cup grated carrots**
- 2 **tablespoons sherry, optional Minced fresh parsley**

1. In a Dutch oven, cook bacon over medium heat until crisp. Using a slotted spoon, remove to paper towels to drain. In the drippings, saute the celery, onion and green pepper until tender.
2. Stir in flour and pepper until blended; gradually add broth and milk. Bring to a boil; cook and stir for 1-2 minutes or until thickened.
3. Add the cheese, olives, carrots and sherry if desired; cook and stir until cheese is melted. Sprinkle servings with parsley and bacon.

CHEESE SOUP WITH A TWIST

Mexican Chicken Tortilla Chowder

Your guests will think you picked this soup up from a restaurant. It's your little secret how easy it is to make.
—**DANA ROOD** OREANA, IL

START TO FINISH: 30 MIN.
MAKES: 10 SERVINGS (2½ QUARTS)

- 2 cans (10¾ ounces each) condensed cream of potato soup, undiluted
- 2 cans (10¾ ounces each) condensed cream of chicken soup, undiluted
- 2 cups 2% milk
- 1 can (14½ ounces) reduced-sodium chicken broth
- 1 can (11 ounces) Mexicorn, drained
- 1 package (9 ounces) ready-to-serve roasted chicken breast strips, chopped
- 1 can (4 ounces) chopped green chilies
- 3 flour tortillas (8 inches), cut into 2-inch x ½-inch strips
- 1 cup (4 ounces) shredded cheddar cheese
  Additional shredded cheddar cheese, optional

In a large saucepan, combine the soups, milk and broth. Heat through, stirring frequently. Add the corn, chicken and chilies; bring to a boil. Stir in tortilla strips. Reduce heat; simmer, uncovered, for 5 minutes. Stir in cheese until melted. Sprinkle each serving with additional cheese if desired.

SUE'S CREAM OF BAKED POTATO SOUP

Sue's Cream of Baked Potato Soup

Nothing beats a good baked potato soup recipe. Serve it with a crusty bread and crisp salad to complete the meal.
—**SUE SHEPARD** TERRYTOWN, LA

PREP: 1¼ HOURS • **COOK:** 20 MIN.
MAKES: 7 SERVINGS

- 3 medium potatoes
- 6 bacon strips, chopped
- 1 large onion, chopped
- 3 garlic cloves, minced
- 1 can (14½ ounces) chicken broth
- 1 can (10¾ ounces) condensed cream of chicken soup, undiluted
- 1 can (5 ounces) evaporated milk
- 1 package (8 ounces) process cheese (Velveeta), cubed
- 1 cup 2% milk
- ¼ cup butter, cubed
- 1 teaspoon dried basil
- ⅛ teaspoon pepper
  Shredded cheddar cheese

1. Scrub and pierce potatoes. Bake at 400° for 50-60 minutes or until tender.
2. Meanwhile, in a large saucepan, cook bacon over medium heat until crisp. Remove to paper towels with a slotted spoon; drain grease from pan, reserving 2 tablespoons drippings. Set aside bacon.
3. Saute onion in drippings until tender. Add garlic; cook 1 minute longer. Stir in the broth, soup and evaporated milk. Bring to a gentle boil. Remove pulp from potatoes; stir into soup mixture. Discard potato shells.
4. Cool slightly. In a blender, process half of the soup until smooth. Return to pan. Add the process cheese, 2% milk, butter, basil and pepper; cook and stir until cheese is melted. Sprinkle servings with cheddar cheese and bacon.

Sweet Potato Soup

Ginger and peanut butter flavor make this dazzling orange soup unique. It has a mild, not spicy, taste with an Asian flair.

—HILDA FALLAS KIRKLAND, WA

PREP: 25 MIN. • **COOK:** 20 MIN.
MAKES: 8 SERVINGS (2 QUARTS)

- 1 large onion, chopped
- 1 medium sweet red pepper, chopped
- 2 medium carrots, chopped
- 2 teaspoons canola oil
- 1 teaspoon minced fresh gingerroot
- 1 garlic clove, minced
- ½ teaspoon cayenne pepper
- ½ teaspoon coarsely ground pepper
- 1 carton (32 ounces) plus 1 can (14½ ounces) reduced-sodium chicken broth
- 1 can (14½ ounces) diced tomatoes, undrained
- 1 large sweet potato, peeled and cubed
- ⅔ cup creamy peanut butter
- 2 teaspoons honey
- 4 green onions, chopped

1. In a large saucepan, saute the onion, red pepper and carrots in oil for 3 minutes. Stir in the ginger, garlic, cayenne and pepper; cook 2 minutes longer. Add the broth, tomatoes and sweet potato. Bring to a boil. Reduce heat; cover and simmer for 15-20 minutes or until potatoes are tender.

2. Cool slightly. In a blender, cover and process soup in batches until smooth. Return all to pan and heat through. Stir in peanut butter and honey. Cook and stir until peanut butter is melted. Garnish servings with green onions.

Scallop & Shrimp Chowder

Dare to go different with this chowder—shrimp and scallops make it feel extra-special. Toss some crispy bacon on for a classic garnish.

—TASTE OF HOME TEST KITCHEN

PREP: 15 MIN. • **COOK:** 20 MIN.
MAKES: 6 SERVINGS

- 6 bacon strips, chopped
- 2 celery ribs, finely chopped
- ½ cup chopped sweet orange pepper
- 1 small onion, finely chopped

- 2 garlic cloves, minced
- ¼ cup all-purpose flour
- 1 can (14½ ounces) chicken broth
- 2 cups 2% milk
- 2 medium red potatoes, cubed
- 1 teaspoon seafood seasoning
- ¼ teaspoon salt
- ½ pound uncooked medium shrimp, peeled and deveined
- ½ pound bay scallops
- 1½ cups (6 ounces) shredded cheddar cheese

1. In a large saucepan, cook bacon over medium heat until crisp. Remove to paper towels with a slotted spoon; drain grease from pan, reserving 2 tablespoons drippings.

2. In the drippings, saute the celery, orange pepper and onion until crisp-tender. Add garlic; cook 1 minute longer. Stir in flour until blended; gradually add broth and milk. Bring to a boil; cook and stir for 1 minute or until thickened.

3. Add the potatoes, seafood seasoning and salt; return to a boil. Reduce heat; cover and simmer for 10-15 minutes or until potatoes are tender.

4. Add shrimp and scallops; cook and stir for 3-4 minutes or until shrimp turn pink and scallops are opaque. Stir in cheese until melted. Garnish each serving with bacon.

SWEET POTATO SOUP

Basil-Onion Cream Soup

My father-in-law introduced me to this soup. It dresses up any meal, and it's always my first choice when I am making a special dinner for friends or family.

—**MELISSA KOEHLER** WAUSAU, WI

START TO FINISH: 25 MIN.
MAKES: 6 SERVINGS

- 2 **medium onions, chopped**
- ¼ **cup butter**
- 2 **tablespoons canola oil**
- 6 **tablespoons all-purpose flour**
- 6 **cups chicken broth**
- 1 **cup heavy whipping cream**
- ⅓ **cup minced fresh basil or**
  2 tablespoons dried basil
  Salt and pepper to taste

In a large saucepan, saute onions in butter and oil. Stir in flour until blended; gradually add broth. Bring to a boil; cook and stir for 2 minutes or until thickened. Stir in cream and basil. Season with salt and pepper. Heat through.

Chorizo Sausage Corn Chowder

The spiciness of the sausage is a wonderful counterpart to the corn's sweetness. Let this soup warm you up.

—**ROBIN HAAS** CRANSTON, RI

PREP: 25 MIN. • **COOK:** 20 MIN.
MAKES: 6 SERVINGS (2½ QUARTS)

- 3 **cups frozen corn, thawed**
- 1 **large onion, chopped**
- 1 **celery rib, chopped**
- 1 **teaspoon olive oil**
- 2 **garlic cloves, minced**
- 3 **cans (14½ ounces each)**
  reduced-sodium chicken broth
- 1 **tablespoon sherry or additional**
  reduced-sodium chicken broth
- 2 **bay leaves**
- 1 **teaspoon dried thyme**
- ½ **teaspoon pepper**
- 1 **package (12 ounces) fully cooked**
  chorizo chicken sausage or flavor
  of your choice, chopped
- 1 **cup half-and-half cream**
- 1 **cup (4 ounces) shredded smoked**
  Gouda cheese
- 1 **medium sweet red pepper, chopped**
- 2 **green onions, chopped**

1. In a nonstick Dutch oven coated with cooking spray, saute the corn, onion and celery in oil until tender. Add garlic; cook 1 minute longer. Stir in the broth, sherry, bay leaves, thyme and pepper. Bring to a boil. Reduce heat; simmer, uncovered, for 8-10 minutes. Discard bay leaves.

2. Cool slightly. In a food processor, process soup in batches until blended. Return all to pan. Stir in sausage and cream; heat through. Sprinkle with cheese, red pepper and green onions.

Jazzed-Up Clam Chowder

No one ever guesses that my dressed-up and delicious chowder starts with canned ingredients! It takes only 10 minutes to put together.

—**JOSEPHINE PIRO** EASTON, PA

START TO FINISH: 10 MIN.
MAKES: 4 SERVINGS

- 1 **can (19 ounces) chunky New**
  England clam chowder
- 1 **can (8¼ ounces) cream-style corn**
- ⅔ **cup 2% milk**
- 2 **tablespoons shredded cheddar**
  cheese
- 2 **tablespoons bacon bits**
- 2 **tablespoons minced chives**

In a 1½-quart microwave-safe dish, combine the clam chowder, corn and milk. Cover and microwave on high for 4-6 minutes or until heated through, stirring every 2 minutes. Sprinkle servings with cheese, bacon and chives.

NOTE *This recipe was tested in a 1,100-watt microwave.*

Favorite Fennel Soup

For an interesting first course, try this delicate soup. The light broth has a mild fennel taste.

—**NANETTE CHERAMIE** OKLAHOMA CITY, OK

PREP: 15 MIN. • **COOK:** 40 MIN.
MAKES: 5 SERVINGS

- 4 **fennel bulbs, sliced**
- 1 **large onion, chopped**
- 2 **tablespoons butter**
- 2 **cans (14½ ounces each)**
  vegetable or chicken broth
- 2 **cups milk**
- 1 **bay leaf**
  Salt and pepper to taste
- 2 **egg yolks**
- ½ **cup half-and-half cream**

1. In a large saucepan, saute fennel and onion in butter until tender. Add the broth, milk and seasonings. Cover and simmer for 30 minutes. Strain, reserving broth. Discard fennel, onion and bay leaf.

2. In a small bowl, beat egg yolks and cream. Gradually add a small amount of hot soup. Return all to the pan. Cook and stir until slightly thickened. Simmer 10-15 minutes longer (do not boil).

JAZZED-UP CLAM CHOWDER

Cream of Tomato Soup

Even folks who don't like tomato soup like this recipe. It's awesome with the seasoned homemade oyster crackers.
—**LINDA PARKHURST** BROOKLYN, MI

START TO FINISH: 30 MIN.
MAKES: 9 SERVINGS (3 CUPS CRACKERS)

- 1 **can (14½ ounces) stewed tomatoes**
- 4 **ounces cream cheese, cubed**
- 1 **medium onion, chopped**
- 2 **garlic cloves, minced**
- ¼ **cup butter**
- 3 **cans (10¾ ounces each) condensed tomato soup, undiluted**
- 2 **cans (11½ ounces each) V8 juice**
- 1 **cup half-and-half cream**
- ½ **teaspoon dried basil**

SEASONED OYSTER CRACKERS

- 3 **cups oyster crackers**
- ⅓ **cup canola oil**
- 1 **tablespoon ranch salad dressing mix**
- ½ **teaspoon garlic powder**
- ½ **teaspoon dill weed**
- 9 **tablespoons shredded part-skim mozzarella cheese**

1. In a food processor, combine stewed tomatoes and cream cheese; cover and process until smooth. Set aside.

2. In a large saucepan, saute onion and garlic in butter. Whisk in tomato soup and V8 until blended. Gradually stir in the cream cheese mixture, cream and basil. Cook and stir until heated through (do not boil).

3. In a large bowl, combine the crackers, oil, dressing mix, garlic powder and dill; toss to coat. Ladle soup into bowls; sprinkle with crackers and mozzarella cheese.

Cheddar Broccoli Soup

This recipe calls for frozen broccoli, which definitely speeds up your prep time.
—**LOUISE BEATTY** AMHERST, NY

START TO FINISH: 30 MIN.
MAKES: 4 SERVINGS

- 1 **small onion, chopped**
- 2 **garlic cloves, minced**
- 2 **tablespoons butter**
- 2 **tablespoons all-purpose flour**
- 1 **can (14½ ounces) beef broth**
- 1½ **cups 2% milk**
- 1 **package (10 ounces) frozen chopped broccoli**
- 1 **teaspoon ground mustard**
- 1 **teaspoon Worcestershire sauce**
- ¼ **teaspoon ground nutmeg**
- 1 **cup (4 ounces) shredded cheddar cheese**

1. In a large saucepan, saute onion and garlic in butter until tender. Stir in flour until blended. Gradually stir in broth; bring to a boil. Cook and stir for 2 minutes.

2. Stir in the milk, broccoli, mustard, Worcestershire sauce and nutmeg. Bring to a boil. Reduce heat; simmer, uncovered, for 6-8 minutes or until heated through. Stir in cheddar until melted.

Ground mustard (also called **dry mustard**) is made from finely ground mustard seeds.

Parmesan Artichoke Soup

This unique cream soup boasts a fantastic combination of artichokes, sun-dried tomatoes and Parmesan cheese.

—**MALEE JERGENSEN** MURRAY, UT

PREP: 25 MIN. • **COOK:** 30 MIN.
MAKES: 12 SERVINGS (3 QUARTS)

- 4 celery ribs, finely chopped
- 1 medium onion, finely chopped
- ½ cup finely chopped carrot
- ½ cup butter, cubed
- 3 garlic cloves, minced
- 1 cup all-purpose flour
- 4½ teaspoons minced fresh thyme or 1½ teaspoons dried thyme
- ¾ teaspoon salt
- ½ teaspoon pepper
- 2 cartons (32 ounces each) reduced-sodium chicken broth
- 3 bay leaves
- 1 quart heavy whipping cream
- 1½ cups shredded Parmesan cheese
- 1 jar (7½ ounces) marinated quartered artichoke hearts, drained and coarsely chopped
- ¼ cup sun-dried tomatoes (not packed in oil), chopped

1. In a large saucepan, saute the celery, onion and carrot in butter until tender. Add garlic; cook 1 minute longer. Stir in the flour, thyme, salt and pepper until blended; gradually add broth. Add bay leaves. Bring to a boil. Cook and stir for 2 minutes or until thickened.

2. Reduce heat; whisk in the cream, cheese, artichokes and tomatoes. Bring to a gentle boil. Simmer, uncovered, for 5-10 minutes or until flavors are blended. Discard bay leaves.

BASIL TOMATO SOUP WITH ORZO

The soup is so delicious that it's completely worth the time it takes to cut up the fresh basil. I believe it is even better the next day, after the flavors have a chance to blend in the refrigerator.

—**TONIA BILLBE** ELMIRA, NY

Basil Tomato Soup with Orzo

PREP: 15 MIN. • **COOK:** 25 MIN.
MAKES: 16 SERVINGS (4½ QUARTS)

- 1 large onion, chopped
- ¼ cup butter, cubed
- 2 garlic cloves, minced
- 3 cans (28 ounces each) crushed tomatoes
- 1 carton (32 ounces) chicken broth
- 1 cup loosely packed basil leaves, chopped
- 1 tablespoon sugar
- ½ teaspoon pepper
- 1¼ cups uncooked orzo pasta
- 1 cup heavy whipping cream
- ½ cup grated Romano cheese

1. In a Dutch oven, saute onion in butter for 3 minutes. Add garlic; cook 1-2 minutes longer or until onion is tender. Stir in the tomatoes, broth, basil, sugar and pepper. Bring to a boil. Reduce heat; cover and simmer for 15 minutes.

2. Meanwhile, cook the orzo according to package directions; drain. Add orzo and cream to soup; heat through (do not boil). Sprinkle servings with cheese.

Curried Parsnip Soup

My mum used to make this recipe at home in England, where parsnips are more widely used than in America. Give it a try—the soup gets a little punch from the curry and pepper.

—**JULIE MATHIESON** BRISTOL, TN

PREP: 15 MIN. • **COOK:** 35 MIN.
MAKES: 6 SERVINGS

- 1 large onion, chopped
- 1 large carrot, chopped
- 1 tablespoon butter
- 1 pound parsnips, peeled and chopped
- 2 cans (14½ ounces each) reduced-sodium chicken broth
- 1 teaspoon curry powder
- ¼ teaspoon salt
- ¼ teaspoon pepper
- 1 cup fat-free milk

1. In a large saucepan, saute onion and carrot in butter until onion is tender. Add parsnips; cook 2 minutes longer. Stir in broth and seasonings. Bring to a boil. Reduce heat; cover and simmer for 12-15 minutes or until parsnips are tender.
2. Cool slightly. In a blender, process soup in batches until smooth. Return all to the pan; stir in milk and heat through.

Creamy Carrot Soup

I first sampled this carrot soup at a local Victorian tea room and wouldn't leave until I had the recipe in hand. The chef was kind enough to share it with me so I could enjoy it at home.

—**CAROLE MARTIN** COFFEEVILLE, MS

PREP: 10 MIN. • **COOK:** 50 MIN.
MAKES: 4-5 SERVINGS

- ¾ cup chopped onion
- 3 tablespoons butter, divided
- 3 cups chopped carrots
- 3 cups chicken broth
- 2 tablespoons uncooked long grain rice
- ½ cup heavy whipping cream
- 1 to 2 tablespoons tomato paste
- ½ teaspoon salt
- ¼ teaspoon white pepper

1. In a large saucepan, saute the onion in 2 tablespoons butter. Add the carrots, broth and rice. Bring to a boil. Reduce heat; cover and simmer for 25 minutes or until carrots and rice are tender. Cool slightly.
2. Transfer to a blender; cover and process until smooth. Return to pan. Add the cream, tomato paste, salt, pepper and remaining butter; heat through.

Halibut Chowder

Several times a year I invite both my retired and current teaching friends to a dinner party with their spouses. I've served this halibut chowder at those parties, and it's a big hit.

—**TERESA LUECK** ONAMIA, MN

PREP: 25 MIN. • **COOK:** 30 MIN.
MAKES: 12 SERVINGS (3 QUARTS)

- 4 celery ribs, chopped
- 3 medium carrots, chopped
- 1 large onion, chopped
- ½ cup butter, cubed
- ½ cup all-purpose flour
- ¼ teaspoon white pepper
- 2 cups 2% milk
- 1 can (14½ ounces) chicken broth
- ¼ cup water
- 1 tablespoon chicken base
- 3 medium potatoes, peeled and chopped
- 1 can (15¼ ounces) whole kernel corn, drained
- 3 bay leaves
- 2 cups half-and-half cream
- 2 tablespoons lemon juice
- 1 pound halibut or other whitefish fillets, cut into 1-inch pieces
- 1 cup salad croutons
- ¾ cup grated Parmesan cheese
- ½ cup minced chives

1. In a large saucepan, saute the celery, carrots and onion in butter until tender. Stir in flour and pepper until blended; gradually add the milk, broth, water and chicken base. Bring to a boil; cook and stir for 2 minutes or until thickened.
2. Add the potatoes, corn and bay leaves. Return to a boil. Reduce heat; cover and simmer for 15-20 minutes or until potatoes are tender.
3. Stir in cream and lemon juice; return to a boil. Add halibut. Reduce heat; simmer, uncovered, for 7-11 minutes or until fish flakes easily with a fork. Discard bay leaves.
4. Garnish servings with croutons, cheese and chives.
NOTE *Look for chicken base near the broth and bouillon.*

CURRIED PARSNIP SOUP

CRAB CORN CHOWDER

Crab Corn Chowder

Don't have time to make a homemade soup? Think again! Canned corn and crab blend beautifully in this creamy, colorful soup, and you'll be ladling it up in no time.
—**SARAH MCCLANAHAN** RALEIGH, NC

START TO FINISH: 25 MIN.
MAKES: 8 SERVINGS

- 3 **teaspoons chicken bouillon granules**
- 2 **cups boiling water**
- 6 **bacon strips, diced**
- ⅓ **cup each diced sweet red, yellow and orange peppers**
- ½ **cup chopped onion**
- ¼ **cup all-purpose flour**
- 3 **cups half-and-half cream**
- 2 **cans (14¾ ounces each) cream-style corn**
- 1½ **teaspoons seasoned salt**
- ½ **teaspoon dried basil**
- ¼ **to ½ teaspoon cayenne pepper**
- 2 **cans (6 ounces each) crabmeat, drained, flaked and cartilage removed, or 2 cups imitation crabmeat, flaked**
- ½ **cup minced chives**

1. Dissolve bouillon in water; set aside. In a Dutch oven, cook bacon over medium heat until crisp. Remove bacon to paper towels to drain, reserving drippings.

2. In the same pan, saute peppers and onion in drippings until tender. Stir in flour. Gradually stir in bouillon. Bring to a boil; cook and stir for 2 minutes or until thickened.

3. Reduce heat; gradually stir in cream and corn. Add the seasoned salt, basil and cayenne. Cook for 8-10 minutes or until heated through, stirring occasionally (do not boil).

4. Stir in the crab. Garnish each bowl with bacon and chives.

Coconut Shrimp Chowder

After eating coconut soup at a Thai restaurant, I added coconut milk to my fish chowder recipe—it was perfect! The fresh, simple ingredients allow the seafood to shine.

—**MICHALENE BASKETT** DECATUR, GA

START TO FINISH: 30 MIN.
MAKES: 5 SERVINGS

- 1 medium onion, chopped
- 2 teaspoons canola oil
- ¼ teaspoon cayenne pepper
- 2 cups chicken broth
- 1 package (10 ounces) frozen corn
- ¼ teaspoon salt
- ¼ teaspoon pepper
- 1 can (13.66 ounces) coconut milk
- 1 pound uncooked medium shrimp, peeled and deveined
- ¼ cup lime juice
- 2 tablespoons minced fresh cilantro
- 1 medium ripe avocado, peeled and cubed

1. In a large saucepan, saute onion in oil until tender. Add pepper. Stir in the broth, corn, salt and pepper. Bring to a boil. Reduce heat; simmer, uncovered, for 5 minutes. Remove from the heat and stir in coconut milk. Cool slightly.

2. In a food processor, process soup in batches until blended. Return all to pan. Add shrimp; cook and stir over medium heat for 5-6 minutes or until shrimp turn pink. Stir in lime juice and cilantro. Garnish servings with avocado.

Hungarian Mushroom Soup

You can imagine you are eating at a fine restaurant when you try this cream soup; it's that tasty.

—**SANDY VAUGHN** CENTRAL POINT, OR

PREP: 20 MIN. • **COOK:** 30 MIN.
MAKES: 4 SERVINGS

- 1 large sweet onion, chopped
- ¼ cup butter, cubed
- ¾ pound sliced fresh mushrooms
- 3 tablespoons all-purpose flour
- 1 tablespoon paprika
- 1 teaspoon dill weed
- ¾ teaspoon salt
- ¼ teaspoon coarsely ground pepper
- 1 can (14½ ounces) chicken broth
- 1 cup 2% milk
- 1 tablespoon soy sauce
- ½ cup sour cream
- 2 teaspoons lemon juice

1. In a large saucepan, saute onion in butter for 2 minutes. Add mushrooms; cook 4-5 minutes longer or until mushrooms are tender.

2. Stir in the flour, paprika, dill, salt and pepper until blended. Gradually stir in the broth, milk and soy sauce. Bring to a boil; cook and stir for 2 minutes or until thickened. Reduce heat; cover and simmer for 15 minutes.

3. Just before serving, stir in sour cream and lemon juice (do not boil).

COCONUT SHRIMP CHOWDER

Soups for Two

102 98 97

Not expecting a big crowd tonight? No problem. These **scaled-down** soups are ideal for a relaxing dinner at home. Better yet, you can easily double or triple the ingredients if necessary to **welcome guests** who stop by. We call that a **win-win!**

BEST CHICKEN TORTILLA SOUP

5. Cut chicken into strips and add to soup; heat through. Discard bay leaf. Garnish with the avocado, cheese and tortilla strips.

NOTE *Wear disposable gloves when cutting hot peppers; the oils can burn skin. Avoid touching your face.*

Chili with Corn Bread Topping

Corn bread and chili just belong together, and this recipe proves it! You can have this on the table in less than 40 minutes.
—TASTE OF HOME TEST KITCHEN

PREP: 20 MIN. • **BAKE:** 15 MIN.
MAKES: 2 SERVINGS

- ⅓ **pound lean ground beef (90% lean)**
- ¼ **cup chopped onion**
- 1 **can (15 ounces) chili with beans**
- ½ **cup water**
- ¾ **cup corn bread/muffin mix**
- 3 **tablespoons 2% milk**
- 2 **tablespoons beaten egg**
- ⅓ **cup shredded cheddar cheese**
- ¼ **cup frozen corn, thawed**

1. In a large skillet, cook beef and onion over medium heat until meat is no longer pink; drain. Stir in chili and water. Bring to a boil. Reduce heat; cover and simmer for 10 minutes. Pour into two 2-cup baking dishes.
2. In a small bowl, combine the corn bread mix, milk and egg. Stir in cheese and corn just until combined. Spread batter evenly over chili.
3. Bake at 400° for 15-18 minutes or until topping is golden brown.

Best Chicken Tortilla Soup

Grilled chicken and veggies add a certain richness to a soup perfect for using up garden-fresh bounty.
—KATHY AVERBECK DOUSMAN, WI

PREP: 30 MIN. • **COOK:** 25 MIN.
MAKES: 3 SERVINGS

- 2 **medium tomatoes**
- 1 **small onion, cut into wedges**
- 1 **garlic clove, peeled**
- 4 **teaspoons canola oil, divided**
- 1 **boneless skinless chicken breast half (6 ounces)**
- ¼ **teaspoon lemon-pepper seasoning**
- ⅛ **teaspoon salt**
- 2 **corn tortillas (6 inches)**
- ½ **cup diced zucchini**
- 2 **tablespoons chopped carrot**
- 1 **tablespoon minced fresh cilantro**
- ¾ **teaspoon ground cumin**
- ½ **teaspoon chili powder**
- 1 **cup reduced-sodium chicken broth**
- ½ **cup spicy hot V8 juice**
- ⅓ **cup frozen corn**
- 2 **tablespoons tomato puree**
- 1½ **teaspoons chopped seeded jalapeno pepper**
- 1 **bay leaf**
- ¼ **cup cubed or sliced avocado**
- ¼ **cup shredded Mexican cheese blend**

1. Brush the tomatoes, onion and garlic with 1 teaspoon oil. Broil 4 in. from the heat for 6-8 minutes or until tender, turning once. Peel and discard charred skins from tomatoes; place tomatoes in a blender. Add onion and garlic; cover and process vegetables for 1-2 minutes or until smooth.
2. Sprinkle chicken with lemon-pepper and salt; broil for 5-6 minutes on each side or until a thermometer reads 170°. Cut one tortilla into ¼-in. strips; coarsely chop the remaining tortilla.
3. In a large saucepan, heat remaining oil. Fry tortilla strips until crisp and browned; remove tortilla strips with a slotted spoon.
4. In the same pan, cook the zucchini, carrot, cilantro, cumin, chili powder and chopped tortilla over medium heat for 4 minutes. Stir in the tomato mixture, broth, V8 juice, corn, tomato puree, jalapeno and bay leaf. Bring to a boil. Reduce heat; simmer, uncovered, for 20 minutes.

Gazpacho for Two

Healthy vegetables are the basis of this chilled soup. Looking for a kicked-up version? Use spicy V8 juice instead of regular tomato juice.

—TASTE OF HOME TEST KITCHEN

PREP: 20 MIN. + CHILLING
MAKES: 2 SERVINGS

- 2 medium tomatoes, seeded and chopped
- ½ small green pepper, chopped
- ⅓ cup chopped peeled cucumber
- ⅓ cup chopped red onion
- 1⅓ cups reduced-sodium tomato juice
- ¼ teaspoon dried oregano
- ¼ teaspoon dried basil
- ⅛ teaspoon salt
- 1 small garlic clove, minced
  Dash pepper
  Dash hot pepper sauce
- 1 tablespoon minced chives
  Chopped sweet yellow pepper, optional

1. In a large bowl, combine the tomatoes, green pepper, cucumber and onion. In another bowl, combine the tomato juice, oregano, basil, salt, garlic, pepper and pepper sauce; pour over vegetables.

2. Cover and refrigerate for at least 4 hours or overnight. Just before serving, sprinkle with chives and, if desired, yellow pepper.

Hearty Sausage Chili

You'll have a stick-to-the-ribs bowl of chili in no time—it doesn't need to cook for hours! The chili is great with corn bread.

—JEANNIE KLUGH LANCASTER, PA

PREP: 10 MIN. • **COOK:** 25 MIN.
MAKES: 3 SERVINGS

- ½ pound bulk Italian sausage
- 1 small sweet yellow pepper, diced
- 1 small sweet red pepper, diced
- 1 teaspoon canola oil
- 1 to 2 garlic cloves, minced
- 1 can (15 ounces) crushed tomatoes
- ¾ cup hot chili beans
- 2 tablespoons chili sauce
- 2 teaspoons chili powder
- 1 teaspoon ground cumin
  Sour cream, optional

1. In a large saucepan, saute sausage and peppers in oil until meat is no longer pink. Add garlic; cook 1 minute longer. Drain.

2. Stir in the tomatoes, beans, chili sauce, chili powder and cumin. Bring to a boil. Reduce heat; simmer soup, uncovered, for 20 minutes or until heated through. Serve with sour cream if desired.

(5) INGREDIENTS
Mashed Potato Soup

When you have leftover mashed potatoes, put them to good use in this recipe. Top each bowl with chives for a finishing touch.

—DOROTHY BATEMAN CARVER, MA

START TO FINISH: 15 MIN.
MAKES: 3 SERVINGS

- 1 tablespoon chopped onion
- 1 tablespoon butter
- 2 cups milk
- 1½ cups mashed potatoes (prepared with milk and butter)
- ½ teaspoon salt, optional
- ⅛ teaspoon celery salt, optional
- ⅛ teaspoon pepper
- 1 tablespoon minced chives

In a saucepan, saute onion in butter until tender. Add the milk, potatoes, salt and celery salt, if desired, and pepper; heat through. Sprinkle with chives.

HEARTY SAUSAGE CHILI

DILLED POTATO-LEEK SOUP

Creamy Chicken Corn Chowder

My 10-year-old son helped me create this recipe! It's the perfect way to enjoy a quick home-cooked meal.

—TERRIE SOWDERS CARTHAGE, IN

PREP: 10 MIN. • **COOK:** 25 MIN.
MAKES: 2 SERVINGS

- 1 cup chicken broth
- ⅔ cup cubed peeled potato
- ½ cup frozen corn
- ¼ teaspoon minced garlic
- ⅛ teaspoon dried marjoram
- ⅛ teaspoon dried thyme
- ⅛ teaspoon pepper
- 2 tablespoons all-purpose flour
- ⅔ cup 2% milk
- 2 ounces process cheese (Velveeta), cubed
- ⅔ cup cubed cooked chicken breast

1. In a large saucepan, combine the broth, potato, corn, garlic, marjoram, thyme and pepper. Bring to a boil. Reduce heat; cover and simmer for 15-20 minutes or until the potatoes are tender.

2. Combine flour and milk until smooth; gradually add to vegetable mixture. Bring to a boil; cook and stir for 2 minutes or until slightly thickened. Reduce heat; stir in the cheese until melted. Add the chicken; heat through.

If you want to give this soup some garnish, top each serving with herb potato chips and finely shredded leeks.

—AGNES WARD STRATFORD, ON

Dilled Potato-Leek Soup

START TO FINISH: 30 MIN.
MAKES: 3 SERVINGS

- 1 cup sliced leeks (white portion only)
- 1 celery rib, chopped
- 1½ teaspoons butter
- 2 cups chicken broth
- 1½ cups cubed peeled Yukon Gold potatoes

- 1 large carrot, finely chopped
- ½ teaspoon dried thyme
- ¼ teaspoon salt
- ⅛ teaspoon pepper
- ½ cup buttermilk
- 1½ teaspoons snipped fresh dill or ½ teaspoon dill weed
  Herb potato chips and finely shredded leeks, optional

1. In a large saucepan, saute the leeks and celery in butter until tender. Stir in the broth, potatoes, carrot, thyme, salt and pepper. Bring to a boil. Reduce heat; cover and simmer for 10-15 minutes or until vegetables are tender. Cool slightly.

2. Transfer to a blender; cover and process until smooth. Return to the pan. Whisk a small amount of soup into buttermilk; return all to the pan, stirring constantly. Add dill; heat through (do not boil). Garnish with chips and leeks if desired.

LENTIL SOUP FOR THE SOUL

Red Pepper Shrimp Bisque

When you have steak and salad already on the menu, this is the ideal finishing touch. It's great for special dinners because it feels festive—without a lot of work from you.

—STEPHANIE BUTTARS PHOENIX, AZ

START TO FINISH: 25 MIN.
MAKES: 2 SERVINGS

- 1 cup chicken broth
- 1 jar (7 ounces) roasted sweet red peppers, drained
- ½ teaspoon sugar
- ½ teaspoon paprika
- 1 cup coarsely chopped cooked shrimp (6 ounces)
- ½ cup heavy whipping cream
- ¼ cup grated Romano cheese, divided
- ¼ teaspoon salt
- ⅛ teaspoon pepper
  Dash hot pepper sauce

1. In a small saucepan, bring the broth and roasted peppers to a boil. Reduce heat; cover and simmer for 5 minutes. Remove from the heat and cool slightly.
2. Transfer to a blender; cover and process until pureed. Return to the saucepan. Add sugar and paprika; bring to a boil. Reduce heat; simmer, uncovered, for 5 minutes. Add the shrimp, cream, 2 tablespoons cheese, salt, pepper and hot pepper sauce. Cook and stir for 2 minutes or until heated through. Garnish soup with remaining cheese.

RED PEPPER SHRIMP BISQUE

Lentil Soup for the Soul

My boyfriend and I are vegetarians, so I'm constantly on the lookout for new delicious meatless dishes, and we just love this one. You'll want to make this recipe again and again.

—ATHENA RUSSELL FLORENCE, SC

PREP: 20 MIN. • **COOK:** 30 MIN.
MAKES: 3 SERVINGS

- ⅓ cup chopped peeled parsnip
- ⅓ cup diced peeled potato
- ¼ cup chopped green onions
- ¼ cup chopped leek (white portion only)
- ¼ cup chopped carrot
- ¼ cup chopped celery
- 2 teaspoons olive oil
- 1 can (14½ ounces) vegetable broth
- 1 cup no-salt-added diced tomatoes
- ⅓ cup dried lentils, rinsed
- ¼ cup dry red wine or additional vegetable broth
- 1 teaspoon Worcestershire sauce
- 1 bay leaf
- ⅓ cup minced fresh cilantro

1. In a large saucepan, saute the parsnip, potato, onions, leek, carrot and celery in oil for 3 minutes. Add the broth, tomatoes, lentils, wine, the Worcestershire sauce and bay leaf. Bring to a boil. Reduce heat; cover and simmer for 25-30 minutes or until lentils are tender.
2. Just before serving, discard bay leaf; stir in cilantro.

Smooth Carrot Soup

This bright and creamy soup is my son's favorite. I like that it's fast and makes a perfect amount for the two of us when my husband is away at work.

—ROBYN LARABEE LUCKNOW, ON

START TO FINISH: 30 MIN.
MAKES: 3 SERVINGS

- 2 cups chopped carrots
- ¼ cup chopped onion
- 1 tablespoon butter
- 1 can (14½ ounces) chicken broth
- ¼ teaspoon ground ginger
- ½ cup buttermilk

1. In a small saucepan, saute carrots and onion in butter until crisp-tender. Add broth and ginger. Bring to a boil. Reduce heat; cover and simmer for 10-15 minutes or until carrots are very tender. Cool slightly.
2. Puree soup in a blender; return to the pan. Stir in buttermilk; heat soup through (do not boil).

Fish Chowder

My mother originally shared this special recipe with me. It's an easy way to make a batch of traditional chowder that's perfect for two.

—PAT GONET WENHAM, MA

START TO FINISH: 30 MIN.
MAKES: 2 SERVINGS

- 1 bacon strip, diced
- 2 tablespoons chopped onion
- ½ cup water
- 1 medium potato, cubed
- ¼ teaspoon seafood seasoning
  Dash salt and pepper
- 1 haddock, halibut or cod fillet (6 ounces)
- 1 cup 2% milk
- 2 teaspoons butter

1. In a large saucepan, saute bacon and onion until tender. Add the water, potato, seafood seasoning, salt and pepper. Bring to a boil. Reduce heat; place fillet on top.
2. Cover and cook for 15-20 minutes or until fish flakes easily with a fork. Stir in milk and butter; heat through. Flake fish into pieces before serving.

White Chili

This chili for two goes over well at my house. Since I'm also frequently asked to bring it to gatherings, I just double or triple the recipe to make it work.

—CAROL SWAINSTON SHERIDAN, MI

START TO FINISH: 25 MIN.
MAKES: 2 SERVINGS

- 2 green onions, chopped
- 1 to 2 tablespoons chopped seeded jalapeno pepper
- 2 garlic cloves, minced
- 1½ teaspoons plus 1 tablespoon butter, divided
- ¼ teaspoon rubbed sage
- ¼ teaspoon ground cumin
- ⅛ teaspoon ground ginger
- ½ pound boneless skinless chicken breast, cut into 1-inch cubes
- 1 tablespoon all-purpose flour
- 1¼ cups chicken broth
- 2 tablespoons milk
- 1 can (15½ ounces) great northern beans, rinsed and drained
  Shredded cheddar cheese

1. In a skillet, saute the onions, jalapeno and garlic in 1½ teaspoons butter until crisp-tender. Add the sage, cumin and ginger; cook for 1 minute. Add chicken; cook and stir until lightly browned.
2. In a small saucepan, melt remaining butter. Stir in the flour until smooth; gradually add the broth and milk. Bring to a boil; cook and stir 2 minutes or until thickened. Add beans. Pour over the chicken mixture. Cook over medium heat until heated through. Sprinkle cheese on each serving.

NOTE *Wear disposable gloves when cutting hot peppers; the oils can burn skin. Avoid touching your face.*

WHITE CHILI

Asparagus Cheese Soup

Although I come from a large family, I learned to shrink down recipes while I was living with a roommate. I especially enjoy making this soup in the spring.

—**DONALD LAUGHERTY** CONNELSVILLE, PA

START TO FINISH: 25 MIN.
MAKES: 2 SERVINGS

- 2 cups water, divided
- 1 teaspoon chicken bouillon granules
- ¼ teaspoon seasoned salt
- ¼ teaspoon lemon-pepper seasoning
- ¼ teaspoon white pepper
- ¾ pound fresh asparagus spears, trimmed
- 4 slices process American cheese, cut up
- 1 bacon strip, cooked and crumbled

1. In a small skillet, combine 1 cup water, bouillon, the seasoned salt, lemon-pepper and white pepper. Add asparagus. Bring to a boil. Reduce heat; cover and simmer 8-10 minutes or until asparagus is tender. Remove asparagus; cool slightly.

2. Cut off several asparagus tips and set aside. Cut remaining asparagus into larger pieces. Place asparagus pieces and cooking liquid in a blender or food processor; cover and process until smooth. In a saucepan, combine asparagus mixture and remaining water; heat through. Reduce heat; stir in cheese just until melted. Garnish with the bacon bits and the reserved asparagus tips.

April and May are the best months for **buying fresh asparagus.** Look for **firm, straight** asparagus spears with tightly closed, crisp stalks.

Home-Style Potato Soup

I experimented with and tweaked our family soup recipe until I came up with this winning version. The mashed potato flakes help thicken it, and the bacon adds color and crunch.

—**CAROL HENSON** INDEPENDENCE, KS

START TO FINISH: 30 MIN.
MAKES: 2 SERVINGS

- 2 tablespoons finely chopped onion
- 2 tablespoons chopped celery
- 1 teaspoon canola oil
- 2 medium Yukon Gold potatoes, peeled and diced
- 1½ cups water
- ½ teaspoon chicken bouillon granules
- ¼ teaspoon salt
- ¼ teaspoon pepper
- ½ cup 2% milk
- ¼ cup mashed potato flakes
- 1 ounce process cheese (Velveeta), cubed
- 1 bacon strip, cooked and crumbled

In a small saucepan, saute onion and celery in oil until tender. Add the potatoes, water, bouillon, salt and pepper. Bring to a boil. Reduce heat; cover and simmer for 10-12 minutes or until potatoes are tender. Stir in milk and potato flakes; cook and stir 8 minutes longer. Stir in cheese until melted. Sprinkle servings with bacon.

(5) INGREDIENTS
Roasted Tomato Soup with Fresh Basil for Two

Here's a tasty way to use up an abundance of fresh garden tomatoes. The thyme and basil give the soup a fresh taste—so much better than soup from a can!

—**MARIE FORTE** RARITAN, NJ

PREP: 40 MIN. • **COOK:** 5 MIN.
MAKES: 2 SERVINGS

- 1¼ pounds tomatoes (about 4 medium), halved
- 1 small onion, quartered
- 1 garlic clove, peeled and halved
- 1 tablespoon olive oil
- 1 tablespoon minced fresh thyme
- ½ teaspoon salt
- ⅛ teaspoon pepper
- 4 fresh basil leaves
  Salad croutons and additional fresh basil leaves, optional

1. Place the tomatoes, onion and garlic in a greased 15x10x1-in. baking pan; drizzle with oil. Sprinkle with thyme, salt and pepper; toss to coat. Bake at 400° for 25-30 minutes or until tender, stirring once. Cool slightly.

2. In a blender, process the tomato mixture and the basil leaves until blended. Transfer to a large saucepan and heat through. Garnish each bowl of soup with croutons and additional basil if desired.

ROASTED TOMATO SOUP WITH FRESH BASIL FOR TWO

CREAMY BUTTERNUT SQUASH SOUP

Creamy Butternut Squash Soup

I used to live in Australia, where this soup is often served. I had to have the recipe, and now it's one of my family's favorites.
—**TIFFANY POPE** DRAPER, UT

PREP: 15 MIN. • **COOK:** 20 MIN.
MAKES: 2 SERVINGS

- ¼ cup chopped onion
- 1 tablespoon butter
- 3 cups cubed peeled butternut squash
- 1 medium potato, peeled and cubed
- 1½ cups water
- 1½ teaspoons chicken bouillon granules
- ¼ teaspoon salt
  Dash pepper
- ¼ cup evaporated milk

1. In a small saucepan, saute onion in butter until tender. Add squash and potato; cook and stir for 2 minutes. Add the water, bouillon, salt and pepper; bring to a boil. Reduce heat;

cover and simmer for 15-20 minutes or until vegetables are tender.
2. Cool slightly. In a blender, cover and process the soup until smooth. Return to the pan; stir in milk and heat through.

Pretty Pepper Soup

Why eat out when you can eat something so good at home tonight? I often make a bigger batch of this soup for parties.
—**BESSIE HULETT** SHIVELY, KY

START TO FINISH: 30 MIN.
MAKES: 2 SERVINGS

- 1 bacon strip
- 1 large sweet red pepper, chopped
- ¼ cup chopped onion
- 2 garlic cloves, minced
- 1 tablespoon tomato paste
- ⅛ teaspoon paprika
- 3 to 4 drops hot pepper sauce
  Dash cayenne pepper
- 1 cup chicken broth, divided
- 1 tablespoon butter
- 1 tablespoon all-purpose flour

- ½ cup heavy whipping cream
- ¼ teaspoon salt
  Chives and additional chopped red pepper, optional

1. In a large skillet, cook bacon until crisp. Remove to paper towel to drain. To the drippings, add the red pepper, onion and garlic; saute until onion is tender, about 4 minutes. Stir in the tomato paste, paprika, hot pepper sauce and cayenne until well blended. Add ¼ cup broth. Reduce heat; simmer, uncovered, for 5 minutes. Remove from the heat; cool for 10 minutes. Puree in a blender; set aside.
2. In a large saucepan over low heat, melt butter. Stir in the flour; cook and stir for 2 minutes or until thickened. Gradually add remaining broth; bring to a boil over medium heat. Cook and stir for 2 minutes; reduce heat to low.
3. Gradually stir in cream and salt. Add puree; heat through. Crumble bacon over top. Garnish with chives and red pepper if desired.

BART'S BLACK BEAN SOUP FOR TWO

Curry Chicken Soup for Two

Don't be overwhelmed by the ingredient list—this yummy soup is quick and easy to make. Plus, it's a fantastic way to get in your veggies.

—**JANE HACKER** MILWAUKEE, WI

PREP: 20 MIN. • **COOK:** 15 MIN.
MAKES: 2 SERVINGS

- ¼ **pound boneless skinless chicken breasts, cut into ½-inch cubes**
- 1½ **teaspoons canola oil, divided**
- ⅓ **cup chopped onion**
- ¼ **cup chopped carrot**
- ¼ **cup chopped celery**
- ¼ **cup chopped green pepper**
- ½ **cup chopped peeled apple**
- 1 **tablespoon all-purpose flour**
- ⅛ **teaspoon salt**
- 1 **can (14½ ounces) reduced-sodium chicken broth**
- 2 **tablespoons tomato paste**
- 1 **to 1½ teaspoons curry powder**
- ½ **teaspoon ground ginger**
- ⅛ **to ¼ teaspoon crushed red pepper flakes**
- 1 **tablespoon minced fresh parsley**

1. In a large saucepan coated with cooking spray, cook the chicken in ½ teaspoon oil for 4-5 minutes or until juices run clear. Remove the chicken and set aside.

2. In the same saucepan, saute the onion, carrot, celery and green pepper in remaining oil for 4 minutes. Add the apple; cook 2 minutes longer. Combine flour and salt. Sprinkle over vegetable mixture; cook and stir for 1 minute. Gradually stir in broth and tomato paste. Bring to a boil; cook and stir 1-2 minutes longer or until slightly thickened.

3. Stir in the curry, ginger and pepper flakes. Return chicken to saucepan and bring to a boil. Reduce the heat; simmer, uncovered, for 8-10 minutes or until the vegetables are tender. Sprinkle with parsley.

Bart's Black Bean Soup for Two

Every cook can appreciate a fresh, simple soup that's ready in minutes. Just add a salad and dinner rolls or quesadillas for a complete meal that hits the spot.

—**SHARON ULLYOT** LONDON, ON

START TO FINISH: 10 MIN.
MAKES: 2 SERVINGS

- ¾ **cup canned black beans, rinsed and drained**
- ¾ **cup chicken broth**
- ⅓ **cup salsa**
- ¼ **cup whole kernel corn**
- **Dash hot pepper sauce**
- 1 **teaspoon lime juice**
- ½ **cup shredded cheddar cheese**
- 1 **tablespoon chopped green onion**

In a microwave-safe bowl, combine the first five ingredients. Cover and microwave on high for 2 minutes or until heated through. Pour into two serving bowls; drizzle each with lime juice. Sprinkle soup with cheese and green onions.

NOTE *This recipe was tested in a 1,100-watt microwave.*

Salmon Chowder

This chowder is filling but won't weigh you down. I suggest serving it when there's a chill in the air.

—VICKI THOMPSON BRISTOL, NB

PREP: 20 MIN. • **COOK:** 25 MIN.
MAKES: 2 SERVINGS

- 3 tablespoons chopped onion
- 1 small garlic clove, minced
- ⅛ teaspoon dried basil
- ⅛ teaspoon dried thyme
- 1½ teaspoons butter
- 1 cup 2% milk
- ⅔ cup condensed chicken broth, undiluted
- ¼ cup frozen corn
- ¼ cup chopped carrot
- 1 small red potato, cut into ½-inch cubes
- 4½ teaspoons all-purpose flour
- 2 tablespoons cold water
- 1 salmon fillet (4 ounces), cut into 1-inch pieces
- ¼ cup chopped zucchini
- ¼ teaspoon salt
- ⅛ teaspoon pepper
- ¼ cup shredded reduced-fat cheddar cheese

1. In a small saucepan over medium heat, cook and stir the onion, garlic, basil and thyme in butter until onion is tender. Stir in the milk, broth, corn, carrot and potato. Bring to a boil. Reduce heat; cover and simmer for 6-8 minutes or until the vegetables are tender.
2. Combine the flour and water until smooth; stir into onion mixture. Bring to a boil; cook and stir for 2 minutes or until thickened. Reduce heat; add the salmon, zucchini, salt and pepper. Simmer, uncovered, for 3-5 minutes or until fish flakes easily with a fork. Sprinkle with cheese before serving.

Elegant Mushroom Soup

Turn a few ordinary ingredients into a wonderfully delicious soup. My family is delighted whenever they see this simmering on the stove.

—MARJORIE JAEGER ENDERLIN, ND

START TO FINISH: 10 MIN.
MAKES: 2-3 SERVINGS

- 1 large onion, chopped
- ½ pound fresh mushrooms, sliced
- 2 tablespoons butter
- 2 tablespoons all-purpose flour
- ¼ teaspoon pepper
- ⅛ teaspoon salt
- 1 cup milk
- 1 cup chicken broth
- 1 tablespoon minced fresh parsley
  Ground nutmeg, optional
  Sour cream

1. In a large saucepan, saute onion and mushrooms in butter 3 minutes or until onion is tender. Stir in the flour, pepper and salt; gradually add milk and broth. Bring to a boil; cook and stir for 2 minutes or until soup is thickened. Add parsley; add nutmeg if desired.
2. Top individual servings with a dollop of sour cream.

Store parsley **in the freezer** for later. Wash parsley, shake off excess water, then **wrap the bunch** in a paper towel and put it in a resealable freezer bag.

ELEGANT MUSHROOM SOUP

ITALIAN SAUSAGE MINESTRONE FOR TWO

Italian Sausage Minestrone for Two

Shoo away the cold with this no-fuss minestrone. Feeling daring? Substitute a can of butter beans or pinto beans for one of the cans of cannellini beans.

—**ELIZABETH RENTERIA** VANCOUVER, WA

PREP: 20 MIN. + FREEZING
COOK: 1¼ HOURS • **MAKES:** 3 CUPS

- ¼ **pound bulk Italian sausage**
- ⅓ **cup chopped carrot**
- ¼ **cup chopped celery**
- 3 **tablespoons chopped onion**
- 1 **garlic cloves, minced**
- 2¼ **teaspoons olive oil**
- 1¾ **cups reduced-sodium chicken broth**
- ¾ **cup cannellini or white kidney beans, rinsed and drained**
- ¾ **cup undrained fire-roasted diced tomatoes**
- 1 **bay leaf**
- ¾ **teaspoon Italian seasoning**
- ¾ **teaspoon tomato paste**
- ¼ **cup ditalini or other small pasta Shredded or shaved Parmesan cheese**

1. In a Dutch oven, cook sausage over medium heat until no longer pink; drain.

2. In the same pan, saute the carrots, celery, onion and garlic in oil until tender. Stir in broth, beans, tomatoes, bay leaf, Italian seasoning, tomato paste and sausage. Bring to a boil. Reduce heat; cover and simmer for 30 minutes.

3. Stir in ditalini; return to a boil. Reduce heat and cook, uncovered, for 6-8 minutes or until pasta is tender. Serve with cheese.

⑤ INGREDIENTS
Honeydew Soup

With only three ingredients, this fruit soup is the perfect way to start a summertime supper. It's also easy to double when guests drop in.

—**RUTH ANDREWSON** LEAVENWORTH, WA

PREP: 10 MIN. + CHILLING
MAKES: 3 SERVINGS

- 3 **cups cubed honeydew**
- ½ **cup white grape juice**
- 1 **tablespoon sugar**

In a blender, combine all of the ingredients; cover and process until smooth. Transfer to a bowl. Cover and refrigerate until chilled.

⑤ INGREDIENTS
Effortless Broccoli Soup

Want a soup recipe that serves just a few people so you don't have to fuss much? As its name suggests, this broccoli blend is a cinch to fix, and it makes a wonderful meal for two.

—**BETTY VAUGHN** ELKHART, IN

START TO FINISH: 30 MIN.
MAKES: 2 SERVINGS

- ¼ **cup chopped onion**
- 2 **tablespoons butter**
- 2 **cups chopped fresh broccoli**
- 1 **can (14½ ounces) reduced-sodium chicken broth**
- ½ **teaspoon garlic powder**
- ¼ **teaspoon pepper**
- ⅛ **teaspoon salt**
  Sour cream, optional

1. In a large saucepan, saute onion in butter until tender. Add broccoli, broth, garlic powder, pepper and salt. Bring to a boil. Reduce heat; cover and simmer for 10-12 minutes or until broccoli is tender. Cool slightly.

2. In a blender, cover and process soup until smooth. Return to the pan and heat through. Garnish servings with sour cream if desired.

EFFORTLESS BROCCOLI SOUP

Broccoli & Cheese Potato Soup

If I don't have frozen broccoli on hand for this soup, I toss in some frozen spinach or chopped carrots and celery instead.
—**MARY PRICE** YOUNGSTOWN, OH

START TO FINISH: 30 MIN.
MAKES: 3 SERVINGS

- 3 **cups cubed peeled potatoes**
- 1 **medium onion, chopped**
- 2 **garlic cloves, minced**
- 2 **cups reduced-sodium chicken broth**
- 1 **cup water**
  Dash pepper
- ⅛ **teaspoon salt**
- 3 **cups frozen broccoli florets**
- 3 **tablespoons all-purpose flour**
- ⅓ **cup fat-free milk**
- ½ **cup shredded reduced-fat sharp cheddar cheese**
  Minced fresh parsley

1. In a large saucepan, combine the first seven ingredients; bring to a boil. Reduce heat; simmer, covered, 10-15 minutes or until potatoes are tender. Stir in broccoli; return to a boil.

2. In a small bowl, whisk flour and milk until smooth; stir into soup. Cook and stir 2 minutes or until thickened. Remove from heat; cool slightly.

3. Process in batches in a blender until smooth. Return to pan; heat through. Sprinkle servings with cheese and parsley.

Catfish Soup

When I don't feel like messing around with a recipe that makes a bunch of leftovers, this recipe makes just enough. It's a hit at my house!
—**RUBY WILLIAMS** BOGALUSA, LA

PREP: 10 MIN. • **COOK:** 30 MIN.
MAKES: 2 SERVINGS

- 1 **large onion, chopped**
- ¼ **cup chopped celery**
- 4 **garlic cloves, minced**
- 2 **teaspoons vegetable oil**
- 1½ **cups chopped, seeded and peeled tomatoes**
- 1 **cup water**
- 2 **bay leaves**
- 1 **strip orange peel (about 2 inches x 1 inch)**
- 1 **tablespoon minced fresh parsley**
- ¾ **to 1 teaspoon salt**
- ¼ **teaspoon dried thyme**
- ⅛ **teaspoon coarsely ground pepper**
  Dash cayenne pepper
- 1 **catfish fillet or firm whitefish of your choice (about ½ pound), cubed**

1. In a saucepan, saute the onion, celery and garlic in oil for 3 minutes (some onion pieces will be lightly browned). Stir in the tomatoes, water, bay leaves, orange peel, parsley, salt, thyme, pepper and cayenne. Bring to a boil. Reduce heat; cover and simmer for 20 minutes.

2. Stir in catfish; return to a boil. Reduce heat; cover and simmer for 5 minutes or until fish is tender. Discard bay leaves and orange peel.

Mock Chinese Soup

I tried this soup in a restaurant years ago and couldn't get enough of it. It was so delicious, I had to ask for the recipe, and I've been enjoying it at home ever since.
—**MARLENE ROBERTS** MOORE, OK

START TO FINISH: 20 MIN.
MAKES: 2 SERVINGS

- 2 **cups water**
- ½ **cup canned mixed Chinese vegetables, drained**
- ⅓ **cup canned cut green beans, drained**
- 1 **teaspoon chicken bouillon granules**

In a small saucepan, combine all ingredients. Bring to a boil. Reduce heat; simmer, uncovered, for 10-15 minutes or until heated through.

Crouton-Topped Garlic Soup for Two

PREP: 20 MIN. • **COOK:** 40 MIN.
MAKES: 2 SERVINGS

- 10 **garlic cloves, peeled**
- 1½ **teaspoons olive oil**
- 1 **tablespoon butter**
- 1 **large onion, halved and sliced**
- 1¼ **cups reduced-sodium chicken broth**
- 1½ **teaspoons minced fresh thyme or ½ teaspoon dried thyme**
- 1 **bay leaf**
- ½ **cup heavy whipping cream**
CROUTONS
- 1 **cup cubed sourdough bread, crusts removed**
- 1 **tablespoon olive oil**
- ½ **teaspoon minced fresh rosemary or ⅛ teaspoon dried rosemary, crushed**
- ⅛ **teaspoon salt**
- ⅛ **teaspoon pepper**
TOPPINGS
- ¼ **cup Gruyere cheese or shredded Swiss cheese**
- 1 **tablespoon minced fresh parsley**

1. In a small skillet, cook garlic in oil over low heat for 3-5 minutes or until golden brown. Remove from the heat; set aside.

2. In a large saucepan over medium-high heat, cook onions in butter until softened. Reduce heat to medium-low; cook, stirring occasionally, 30 minutes or until deep golden brown. Add the broth, thyme, bay leaf and reserved garlic. Bring to a boil. Reduce heat; cover and simmer for 20 minutes to allow flavors to blend. Stir in cream; heat through. Discard bay leaf.

3. For croutons, place bread in a small bowl. Combine the oil, rosemary, salt and pepper; drizzle over bread and toss to coat. Place in an ungreased 15x10 x1-in. baking pan. Bake at 400° for 15-20 minutes or until golden brown, stirring occasionally.

4. Top with croutons, cheese and parsley.

Pan roasting the garlic gives this soup extra flavor, while a touch of cream lends body. The herbed croutons enhance the soup's taste and add texture, but it's the freshly grated cheese that makes this dish taste like heaven!
—**CAROLYN KUMPE** EL DORADO, CA

CROUTON-TOPPED GARLIC SOUP FOR TWO

General Index

This index lists every recipe by food category, cooking method and/or major ingredient, so you can easily locate the recipes that best suit your tastes.

STEP-by-STEP

GEOGRAPHY

Hills and Mountains

Sabrina Crewe

Illustrated by Andrew Farmer and Shirley Tourret

CHILDREN'S PRESS®

A Division of Grolier Publishing

LONDON • NEW YORK • HONG KONG • SYDNEY

DANBURY, CONNECTICUT

© 1996 Franklin Watts
First American Edition 1997 by
Children's Press, A Division of Grolier Publishing
Sherman Turnpike, Danbury, CT 06816

ISBN: 0 516 20235 9

Library of Congress Cataloging-in-Publication Data
Crewe, Sabrina
Hills and mountains/Sabrina Crewe; illustrated by Andrew Farmer and Shirley Tourret
p. cm.-- (Step-by-step geography)
Summary: Provides a simple overview of how mountains are formed, how their shapes vary and are changed,
mountain weather, the animals and plants that live on them, and more.
1. Mountains--juvenile literature. [1. Mountains.] I. Farmer, Andrew, ill. II. Tourret, Shirley, ill. III. Title. IV.
Series.
GB512.C74   1997
551.4'32--dc20   96-18471
CIP AC

Printed in Dubai

Planning and production by The Creative Publishing Company
Designed by Ian Winton
Edited by Patience Coster
Consultant: Keith Lye

Photographs: Bruce Coleman: page 4, right (Atlantide SDF), 10 (Jules Cowan),
12 (Atlantide SDF), 19 (Rod Williams), 21 (John Murray), 23 (John Waters), 31 (Andy Price);
Oxford Scientific Films: page 15 (Tony Martin); Oxford Scientific Films/Survival Anglia: page 11 (Dieter and
Mary Plage); Robert Harding Picture Library: page 6 (G M Wilkins), 7, 9;
Tony Stone Worldwide: page 16 (Renee Lynn), 22 (Jeremy Horner), 26 (W Rudolph),
29 (Joe Cornish), 30 (Zigy Kalunzy), 4, left.

Contents

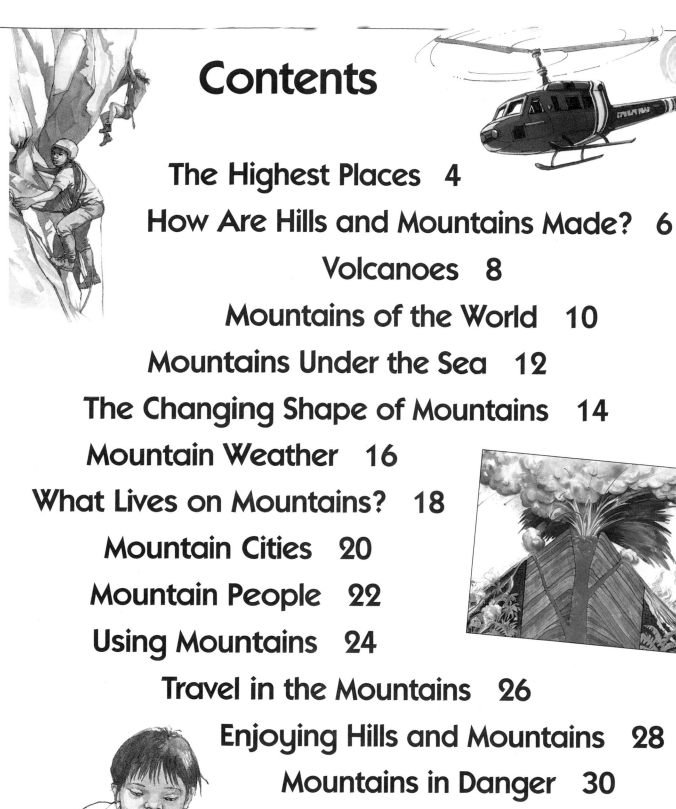

The Highest Places

Have you ever been up a mountain? Are there hills near where you live? If there are, have you climbed them?

What differences can you see between these hills...

...and these mountains?

The hills rise gently above the ground. You can see trees on top of them. These hills would be easy to climb.

The mountains rise steeply; they stand high above the land around them. There are mountains all over the world, even under the sea.

A group of mountains is called a range. Look at this picture. It shows you some of the features of a mountain range.

Peak The sharp point of a mountain

Glacier A mass of ice moving slowly down a mountain and through a valley

Ridge The line along the top of a mountain dividing the valleys on each side

Valley A low area between mountains

Plateau A high but flat piece of land

5

How Are Hills and Mountains Made?

Although we can't usually feel it, the outer layer of the earth is moving all the time. These movements push up huge folds of rock to make hills and mountains. In this photo you can see where the rock has been bent upward.

MAKE SOME MOUNTAINS!

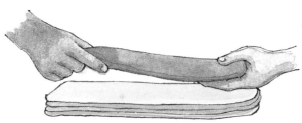

1 Take several pieces of plasticine in different colors and lay them one on top of the other. Press them together.

2 Push the plasticine from each end until it rises up in folds. This is what happens when the earth's surface rises to form mountains.

Hills and mountains take millions of years to form. The biggest **chain** of mountains on land is the Himalayan range in Asia. The Himalayas began to rise over 50 million years ago.

Very old mountains often don't look like mountains at all. They have been worn away over millions of years, and have become much smaller. They are now just hills.

Volcanoes

In some places the outer layer of the earth is thin or weak. Very, very hot liquid rock from deep down inside the earth may push its way up and burst through these weak spots. These exploding mountains are called volcanoes.

When a volcano **erupts**, liquid rock shoots out on to the land. The liquid rock becomes solid as it cools and builds up into a huge mound.

THE VOLCANO THAT BURIED A TOWN

In AD 79, the Italian volcano Vesuvius erupted.

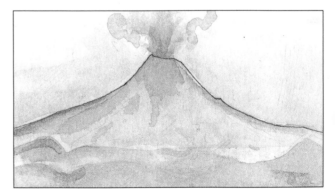

It destroyed the town of Pompeii, covering it in a thick layer of ash.

The volcano in the photo is erupting. You can see a huge cloud of smoke. This is made of gases, ash, steam and lumps of rock.

Archaeologists dug away the ash.

Now you can see the streets and houses of the old town.

Mountains of the World

This world map shows where the longest mountain ranges are. It also shows some famous mountains and volcanoes.

Mount Rushmore in South Dakota has been carved with the giant faces of four American presidents.

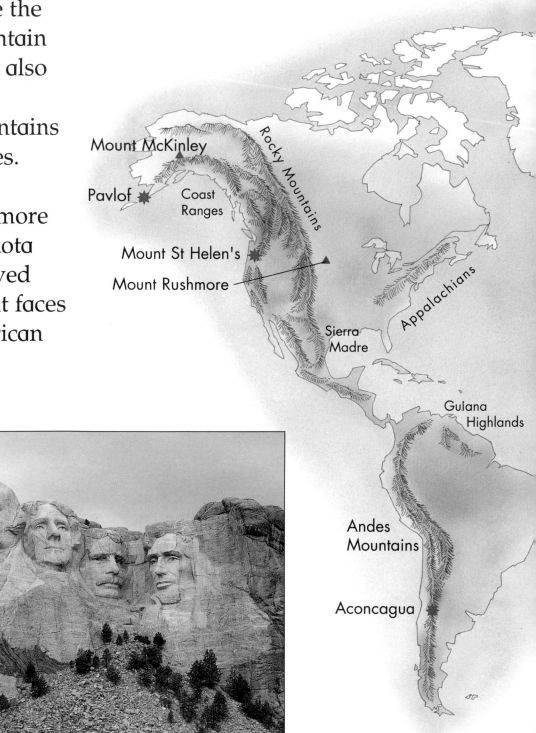

Mount McKinley

Rocky Mountains

Pavlof

Coast Ranges

Mount St Helen's

Mount Rushmore

Sierra Madre

Appalachians

Guiana Highlands

Andes Mountains

Aconcagua

Mount Everest is the highest mountain in the world. It rises 29,028 feet above sea level.

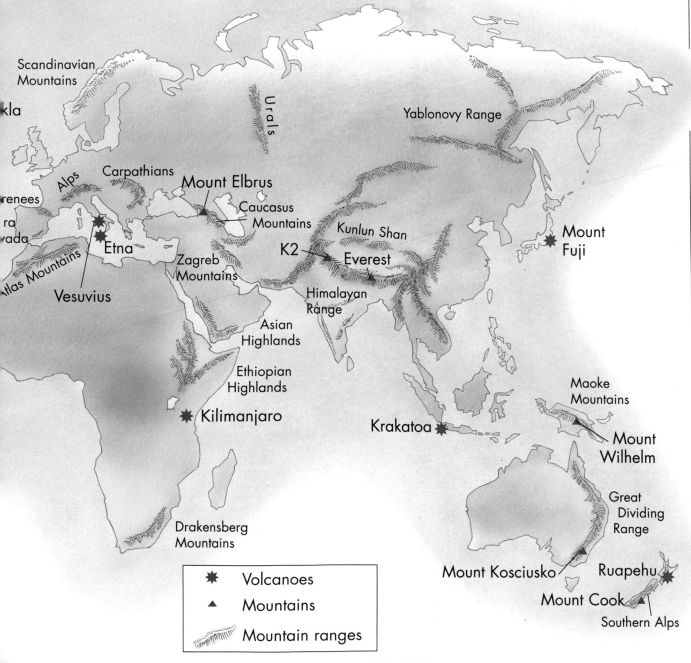

Scandinavian
Mountains

kla

Urals

Yablonovy Range

Carpathians

Alps

Mount Elbrus

renees

ra

ada

Caucasus
Mountains

Kunlun Shan

Mount
Fuji

Etna

K2

Everest

Atlas Mountains

Zagreb
Mountains

Vesuvius

Himalayan
Range

Asian
Highlands

Ethiopian
Highlands

Maoke
Mountains

Kilimanjaro

Krakatoa

Mount
Wilhelm

Great
Dividing
Range

Drakensberg
Mountains

Mount Kosciusko

Ruapehu

Mount Cook

Southern Alps

✺	Volcanoes
▲	Mountains
⋰⋰⋰	Mountain ranges

Mountains Under the Sea

This is the mountain Mauna Kea in Hawaii. It is the tallest mountain in the world, but more than half of Mauna Kea is hidden beneath the sea.

Sometimes the tops of underwater mountains may appear above the water and make islands. The islands of Hawaii are the peaks of a string of volcanoes in the Pacific Ocean.

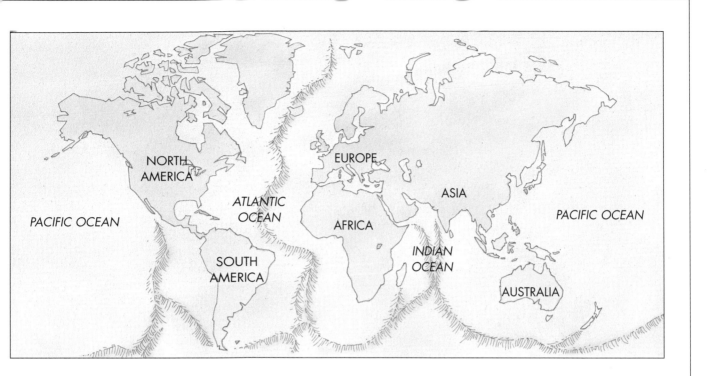

The world's longest range of mountains is hidden underwater. It stretches over 18,500 miles across the Pacific, Atlantic and Indian oceans.

MAKE A WATERY LANDSCAPE

1 Press a large lump of clay into a foil container. Mold the clay into peaks and dips of different shapes and sizes, covering the base of the container with an irregular "landscape."

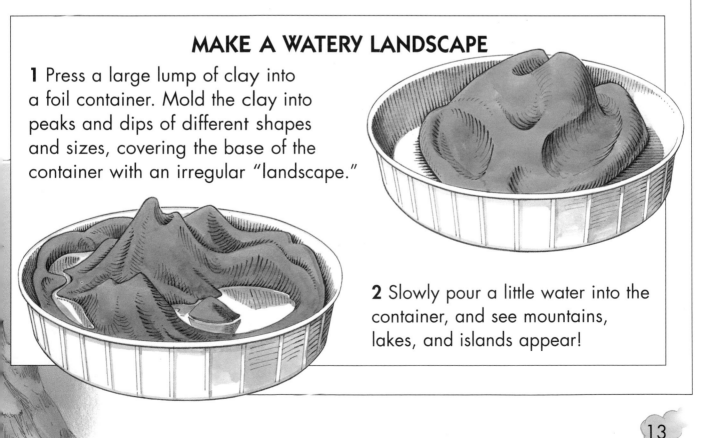

2 Slowly pour a little water into the container, and see mountains, lakes, and islands appear!

The Changing Shape
of Mountains

The shape of a hill or mountain is always changing. The rock is worn away by wind, rain, and water.

Wind blows tiny grains of sand and rock against the mountain and wears it away.

Water collects and freezes between rocks in the mountains. As the water freezes it gets bigger and cracks the rocks. The cracked rock breaks off and is carried away by glaciers and rivers.

High up in the mountains **glaciers** form, where snow builds up and turns into ice. As the ice gets heavier, it flows slowly down the mountain. The glacier makes a deep valley as it moves along.

Rivers carrying small stones wear away the ground and make valleys in the mountain or hillside.

Mountain Weather

Do you know why it is colder at the top of a mountain than at the bottom? At the top there is less **water vapor** and dust in the air. The air is thinner and can't hold so much heat from the sun.

Air grows cooler as it rises

The tops of the highest mountains are always covered in snow. The point where the snow begins is called the snowline. The snowline is very high on Mount Kilimanjaro because it is in a hot country.

Clouds form
and make
rain or snow

Mountains affect the weather. They can cause rain and snow. This is because air rises when it hits a mountain. As it rises, the air becomes cooler and clouds form. The water droplets in the clouds fall as rain or snow.

Dry air blows down the mountain as a warm wind

The air that has passed over the mountain is now much drier and growing warmer. It blows down the other side of the mountain as a warm wind.

What Lives on Mountains?

Few plants and animals live near the tops of high mountains. It is too windy and cold for them to survive.

Nothing grows above the snowline.

Only moss and **lichen** grow on the high, bare rocks.

The point above which no trees can grow is called the "treeline." Above the treeline you can see **alpine plants**. These grow close to the ground so that they are not blown away by the wind.

Below the treeline there are forests.

At the bottom of a mountain, there is often good soil for growing crops.

Some animals have **adapted** to the cold and wind. Mountains goats have thick fur to keep them warm and special hooves for climbing. Eagles have sharp eyes to spot their **prey** as they soar over the mountains. Snow leopards and mountain lions come out of their dens in the day to hunt for animals.

MAKE AN ALPINE GARDEN

1 Ask an adult to make some drainage holes in the base of an old plastic bowl. Put a thick layer of pebbles into it. Fill the bowl with an equal mixture of soil and sand (you will need to buy special coarse sand from a garden store). Place a few small stones on top.

stones

drainage holes

pebbles

soil and sand

2 Plant some alpine plants (heathers, saxifrages, edelweiss) in the soil. Sprinkle a layer of gravel (again available from a garden store) around the plants.

Mountain Cities

Although life in the mountains is hard, people have always settled there. Sometimes they have built towns and cities cut off from the rest of the world. One reason people choose to live in the mountains is because the landscape is so **rugged**. This means that their enemies can't easily attack them.

In the 1200s, the Inca people lived high up in the Andes mountains in South America. They built mountain-top towns and cities and hundreds of miles of roads.

Mountain People

Most of us would feel sick on high mountains because our bodies are not suited to the **altitude**. Mountain people have larger lungs and more red blood cells in their bodies. This means that they can take in more oxygen from the thin air. Protection from wind and cold is provided by their stocky build.

People have always found ways of farming mountainous land. For thousands of years, they have cut **terraces** into the sides of mountains to grow food.

In winter, mountain farmers keep their animals inside. When the snow has melted in summer, the animals are taken up the mountain to graze in high pastures.

Using Mountains

Mountains are useful to us in our daily lives. They provide us with raw materials like wood, metal and stone.

Timber from trees is used for building and for fuel.

In **quarries** stone is dug out of the ground for building houses and roads.

These generators are turning wind into electricity.

Mountain rock is full of **metal ores** that people can use. In this mine, copper is being **extracted** from the ground.

Electricity is made from water at this **hydroelectric plant**. The dam forms a **reservoir**, which supplies water to towns far away.

Travel in the Mountains

People have always had to find ways of crossing mountains.

Ordinary trains can't travel up steep slopes, so special mountain railways and tunnels have to be built.

Only helicopters can reach the most difficult places of all. Mountain rescue teams use helicopters to reach people who are injured or lost in the mountains.

It is impossible to drive a car straight up a mountain, because the slope is too steep. Mountain roads must zigzag to reach the villages high up.

This tunnel has been cut through the mountain rock to make a road for cars. Going around the mountain would make the journey much longer.

27

Enjoying Hills and Mountains

Mountains and hills are among the most beautiful places on earth. All year round many people like to vacation there. In winter, skiers love the thrill of racing over mountain snow.

Climbing and Mountaineering

Mountains attract rock climbers and mountaineers who like to put their skills to the test. Rock climbing is fun, but it can be dangerous. Climbers rope themselves together for safety in case one of them falls.

Expeditions to the highest peaks can last many weeks. Mountaineers take food and equipment to make camps along the way.

In the summer, many people like to hike in clean, fresh air and enjoy the wonderful scenery.

Mountains in Danger

Mountains can be **damaged** by people.

In the valley, land and villages are at risk from flooding.

We all use wood and paper, so trees are cut down to provide us with these. But mountains need trees growing on their slopes to hold the soil in place.

Without trees, the bare soil becomes **eroded**. Soil erosion causes floods and **landslides** below, ruining farmland and houses.

Pollution from cities is carried to the mountains by winds. Pollution causes acid rain which kills trees.

We must look after our hills and mountains if we want to save their land and wildlife.

Many forests have been cut down.

Rainwater washes the bare soil down the mountain.

Earth moving down a bare mountain can cause a landslide.

Glossary

Adapted: To have changed to suit the conditions

Alpine plants: Plants that grow at high altitudes

Altitude: The height of land above sea level

Archaeologists: People who study very old human societies

Chain: A mountain range

Eroded: Worn away

Erupts: Breaks out

Expeditions: Journeys

Extracted: Taken out

Glaciers: Large masses of snow and ice that move down mountains

Hydroelectric plant: A place that makes electricity from water power

Landslide: A mass of loosened rocks and earth sliding down a slope

Lichen: Small moss-like plants that grow in areas when the air is clean

Metal ores: Metal in its natural state

Pollution: Dirty air, water or land

Prey: An animal hunted for food by another animal

Quarries: Places where stone is dug up for human use

Reservoir: A man-made lake

Rugged: Uneven and rough

Terraces: Flat areas of earth with sloping sides, rising one above the other

Water vapor: Invisible moisture in the air

Index